Praise for
The Hedgewitch's Little Book of Crystal Spells

"Most books for solitary practitioners only focus on the use of plants and herbs and almost completely ignore the use of powerful crystals, gems, and minerals that Pachamama/Mother Earth provides us. Tudorbeth arrives to remedy this situation, dividing the crystals according to elemental frequency, and providing spells and elixirs for each available crystal. *The Hedgewitch's Little Book of Crystal Magic* teaches witches in every level to work with each of these precious and unique extensions of the Earth to harness different powers and manifest all kinds of purposes, seeking to strengthen and support your magic and all your goals in the process."

—ELHOIM LEAFAR, author of *Manifestation Magic* and *Dream Witchery*

"*The Hedgewitch's Little Book of Crystal Spells* gives you a profound way to use your crystal allies, paired with Elemental spirits, to boost your magickal techniques and results. Whether you are a new or seasoned witch looking for an easy format to grasp crystal healing magick, Tudorbeth has written it all down for you in a thoughtful and humble way. Packed with an array of crystal varieties and their backstories, from the easily accessible to the rarest ones, you will never fall short in which spells to use no matter what circumstances you are in."

—**CAROL SILVA LIM,** advanced crystal master and cofounder of GemsAwakening

"This little book is absolutely packed with practical, knowledgeable, and simple but very effective uses of the Goddess's gift of crystals. It is an enjoyable, fascinating, and informative read.…Tudorbeth covers how we can use crystals for daily practice (elixirs, cooking, beauty, and health) and there is a crystal that corresponds with every need and situation we come across in life. If the reader already practices magick, Tudorbeth explains how crystals can be added to spells and charms.…The book is full of spells and rituals that all practitioners simply must have to enhance facts, knowledge, and care of these beautiful fruits of the earth.…This is most definitely a book that any self-respecting crystal practitioner needs for their work."

—**BLUEBELL,** crystal and candle magick cottage witch and tarot reader

THE
Hedgewitch's
LITTLE BOOK OF
Crystal Spells

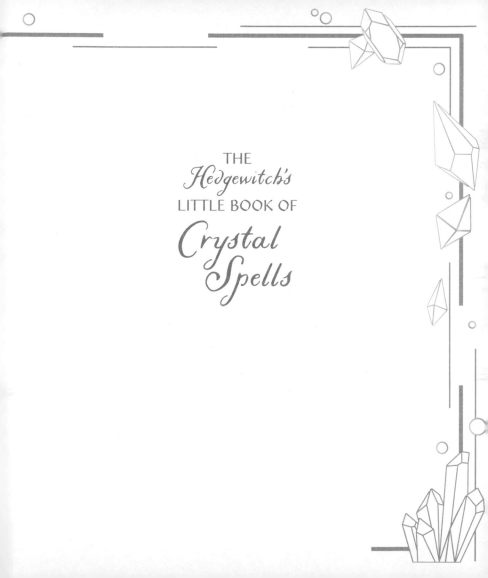

© Sarah Coyne

ABOUT THE AUTHOR

Tudorbeth is the principal of the British College of Witch-craft and Wizardry and teaches courses on witchcraft. She is the author of numerous books, including *A Spellbook for the Seasons* (Eddison Books, 2019). Tudorbeth is a hereditary practitioner; her great grandmother was a well-known tea reader in Ireland while her Welsh great grandmother was a healer and wise woman.

THE
Hedgewitch's
LITTLE BOOK OF
Crystal
Spells

——◆•◆——

TUDORBETH

Llewellyn Worldwide
Woodbury, MN

FIRST EDITION
First Printing, 2024

Book design by Donna Burch-Brown
Cover design by Shira Atakpu
Interior art by the Llewellyn Art Department

Llewellyn Publications is a registered trademark of Llewellyn Worldwide Ltd.

Library of Congress Cataloging-in-Publication Data (Pending)
ISBN: 978-0-7387-7440-4

Llewellyn Publications
A Division of Llewellyn Worldwide Ltd.
2143 Wooddale Drive
Woodbury, MN 55125-2989
www.llewellyn.com

Printed in China

FSC
www.fsc.org
MIX
Paper | Supporting
responsible forestry
FSC™ C007683

OTHER BOOKS BY TUDORBETH

The Hedgewitch's Little Book of Spells, Charms & Brews

The Hedgewitch's Little Book of Seasonal Magic

The Hedgewitch's Little Book of Flower Spells

The Hedgewitch's Little Book of Lunar Magic

—

Llewellyn's 2024 Witches' Companion
(Contributor)

Llewellyn's 2024 Magical Almanac
(Contributor)

Dedication

Dedicated to those who dwell within the pentagram of life;
may we all be protected with your love, light, and power.

Disclaimer

The material contained in this book is for information purposes only. It is not intended to be a medical guide or a manual for self-treatment. The information represented in this book is not a substitute for medical counselling or treatment prescribed by your doctor. It is not intended to diagnose, treat, or cure any diseases, mental health problems, or ailments.

This book is sold with the understanding that the publisher and author are not liable for the misconception, misinterpretation, or misuse of any information provided.

If you have a medical problem, please seek competent professional medical advice and assistance.

Contents

INTRODUCTION 1

The Bare Necessities 7

Crystal Tools 9

How to Use Crystals 12

Where to Find Crystals 17

Key Stones 21

Amber 21

Amethyst 23

Clear Quartz 24

Jet 25

Lapis Lazuli 27

Pearl 28

Rock Salt 30

Rose Quartz 31

Tiger's Eye   32

Turquoise   34

The Quartz Zone 37

Clear Quartz   38

Gateway Quartz   39

Manifestation Quartz   42

Metamorphosis Quartz   43

Phantom Quartz   45

Rose Quartz   46

Smoky Quartz   48

Snow Quartz   49

Crystals of Earth 53

Earth Correspondences   54

Crystals and Spells   54

Bismuth   54

Connemara Marble   56

Desert Rose   58

Falcon's Eye   59

Moss Agate   60

Petrified Wood   62

Poppy Jasper   64

Snakeskin Agate   65

Thunder Egg   66

Turquoise Howlite   68

Other Earth Crystals   69

Mystical Beings: Tree Spirits   75

Featured Stone: Tree Agate   76

Summary   78

Crystals of Fire   79

Fire Correspondences   80

Crystals and Spells   80

Blood Agate   80

Fire Agatc   82

Fire Opal   83

Fulgurite   85

Goldstone   86

Heliodor   87

Lava   89

Orange Aragonite   90

Orange Calcite   91

Vesuvianite   93

Other Fire Crystals   94

Mystical Being: Brighid, the Fire Goddess   99

Featured Stone: Garnet   100

Summary   101

Crystals of Water   103

Water Correspondences   104

Crystals and Spells   104

Aqua Aura   104

Aquamarine   106

Blue Goldstone   107

Blue Jasper   109

Blue Quartz   110

Chlorite Phantom Quartz   112

Ocean Jasper   114

Soapstone   116

Stone of Atlantis   117

Water Agate   119

Other Water Crystals   120

Mystical Beings: Kelpies   125

Featured Stone: Scottish Sapphire   126

Summary   128

Crystals of Air   129

Air Correspondences   130

Crystals and Spells   130

Cloud Agate   130

Haematite   131

Honey Calcite   133

Lodalite   135

Peach Aventurine   137

Peach Moonstone   139

Silver Leaf Agate   140

Tangerine Quartz   142

Yellow Fluorite   144

Yellow Jasper   146

Other Air Crystals   147

Mystical Beings: Air Sprites   152

Featured Stone: Gold Sheen Obsidian   153

Summary   155

Crystals of Spirit   157

Spirit Correspondences   158

Crystals and Spells   158

Angelite   158

Angel Aura   160

Galaxite   161

Meteorite Gibeon   162

Moldavite   164

Nebula Stone   165

Ruby Star   166

Spirit Quartz   168

Star Crystal   169

Star Sapphire   170

White Howlite   171

Other Spirit Crystals   173

Mystical Beings: The Ancients   177

Featured Stone: Merlinite   178
Summary   180

Crystal Divination 181

Gathering and Using the Stones   182
Crystals and Meanings   183
Example Crystal Reading   192
Summary   193

The Last Word 195

APPENDIX OF CRYSTAL SPELLS   197
REFERENCES   203

Introduction

Hedgewitches are curious creatures. They are beings of both worlds, people who seek out elementals while also tending to the matters of a modern life. They can work as teachers, lawyers, chefs, gardeners, receptionists, nurses, and doctors, but all the while they are thinking of that other world they belong to. The hedgewitch practice goes deep within the earth, and magic is in the heart of everything hedgewitches do, and yet no two hedgewitches ever practice the same way.

Hedgewitches are dictated to by their environment; therefore, if they live in a city, their practice will be bound by city parks and recreational places of rest. Museums and galleries will become their places of transportation to the other world in which they reside. For the hedgewitch is a rider of the realms; she lives in the borders that are separated by hedges of brambles or concrete. Thorns and roads are her travelling companions.

One of the old sayings I grew up with was that "witches live at the first house of a village." It is the house on the borders, not quite in the town, but not completely in the forest or the woods. Traditionally, hedgewitches were solitary practitioners of magic, healers of nature, and sorceresses of otherworldly beings. The hedgewitch did not have an earthly family but an elemental one. Think of the hedgewitch as an ambassador to the land of Fae and you will understand what this part of the Craft means.

My series of books, the Hedgewitch's Little Library, aims to show, guide, and teach the practice of a hedgewitch. Each one of these books treads farther down the path of the hedgewitch. We venture deeper along the winding crooked road, covered in honeysuckle and hawthorn, and brush away another layer of magic.

In the first book, *The Hedgewitch's Little Book of Spells, Charms & Brews,* we learned the basics of hedgewitchery, specifically in the five areas of life: love, money, career, family, and health. In the second, *The Hedgewitch's Little Book of Seasonal Magic*, we learned the practical magic that lives within the four seasons of our beautiful planet, with recipes for jams, jellies, tonics, and crafts all combining the power of nature. In the third book, *The Hedgewitch's Little Book of Flower Spells,* we ventured farther down the path by learning the power of flowers and colours. In the fourth, *The Hedgewitch's Little Book of Lunar Magic*, we learned the power, mystery, and lore of the moon.

In each of these books, we learn more about the very nature and practice of hedgewitchery. We learn about the correspondences and how everything is connected, including us. We are connected to each other, to the planet, to this world, and to the next. The correspondences are key to hedgewitchery, and when we understand that, we become the hedgewitch.

The best description of correspondences is to think of the universe as a giant spider's web; every strand and silken thread is connected to something else. When we cast a spell, make a charm or potion, or invoke a power, we tug on one strand, which vibrates many, many others, until countless energies are helping us with our request.

In this book, we are going to venture even farther down that path by looking at crystals. Hedgewitchery and crystals create a perfect pair of magic. There are thousands of crystals, otherwise known as gemstones or semiprecious stones, and all represent the earth, even if they fall from the sky, such as moldavite or meteorite Gibeonite. In that huge spider's web of correspondences, crystals are firmly placed on the earth's strand, and from that strand, they are divided into separate links resonating with their magical intent and purpose. For example, if that magical intent were for passion and physical love, we would use a fire opal in our spell or a vesuvianite, which is an enormously powerful sexual stone found within Mount Vesuvius, which destroyed Pompeii, the echoes of ancient Roman decadence.

Crystals have so many meanings and can be used in every area of our magical practice. In this book, we are going to look at some of the more unusual types of crystals and see their magical intents.

Crystals represent patience, for they have taken hundreds, thousands, millions of years to form. Think of all that energy and power flowing into them that, in turn, we can now use in our magical practice. They are truly a gift to us from the earth itself.

So, let us now begin our journey into the realm of the hedgewitch and tread softly on that path to the magic and wonder of crystals.

The Bare Necessities

Crystals are formed over millions of years with a few exceptions, such as rock salt. They are minerals that grow within the earth and are shaped by volcanic heat and waters. Those crystals that come to us via the universe and crash into our planet are also formed by immense power.

All crystals are markers of time from the very beginning of our earth's birth to present day, and as such, they have ancient energies. They have also witnessed human transformation and have guided and healed us. They hold an ancient connection to our ancestors and are beautiful keepers of our past. Crystals, therefore, have energies flowing through them that are indeed powerful, which we can tap into and utilize.

Their natural forms are found in rocks and meteors. The crystal is formed in nature when molecules or minerals gather together to stabilize during the cooling process. This process is called crystallization, and this can take thousands, even millions of years—for example, each naturally made diamond is over nine hundred million years old, and some are even over three billion years old.[1]

What makes crystals so fascinating and magical is the process called atomic bonding, whereby the atoms and molecules arrange themselves in a repeated three-dimensional pattern. This regular and repeated pattern is the natural process that forms crystals over millions, even billions of years. These crystals can then be turned into gemstones through a process of cutting and faceting. Gemstones are defined by their rarity, beauty, and durability, such as diamonds, rubies, emeralds, and sapphires. However, there are also semiprecious stones, and you will find many of them

---

1. Learn more at https://nature.berkeley.edu/classes/eps2/wisc/Lect6.html.

discussed in this book. The interchangeable terms used to describe these are *crystals* and *semiprecious stones*, which are abbreviated to simply *stones*. In the world today, there are nearly four thousand minerals identified as semiprecious stones and only a handful of gemstones, but all are crystals.

CRYSTAL TOOLS

There are many different magical forms that crystals can take, from wands to spheres to pyramids. My uncle used to make crystal trees, entwined pieces of copper branches whose leaves were amethyst, citrine, quartz, or aventurine, among many others. Each shape overlays with correspondences and meanings. For example, a pyramid is a powerful shape and is often associated with its own magical energies and properties.

Crystal Wands

Crystal wands can be particularly useful in magical practice as they can direct energy to a specific location when used as a pointer. They are also good when working with animals as they offer protection—if the animal were to bite the hand, they would get the crystal wand instead. Crystal wands come in a variety of shapes and sizes, but a good general wand can be held in the palm of your hand.

Crystals Spheres

Crystal spheres are solid round pieces of any form of crystal; common ones are amethyst, aventurine, and quartz. They can also be crystal balls, which are incredibly powerful pieces of equipment and should always be covered by cloth when not in use. Staring into a crystal ball that has first been touched by the enquirer seems to send the fortune teller or scryer into a light trance. Some scryers claim to summon up real scenes from the past, present, or even the future. The relationship between the scryer and the crystal ball can be profound. In this respect, crystal gazing is much like dreaming in that the images seen are essentially symbolic instead of being literal representations.

Crystal Pendulum

Crystal pendulums are excellent scrying tools and are often used for immediate and quick answers to closed questions that require yes-no answers. Crystal pendulums can be anything from a specific pointer-shaped piece of crystal to a favourite crystal ring tied to a piece of ribbon. Make two cards, one saying *yes* and one saying *no*. Hold the crystal pendulum in both your hands and ask your question. Hold the pendulum by the string or ribbon, make sure it is steady and between the two cards, clear your mind, then watch which card the pendulum swings to; that is your answer.

Crystal Eggs

Crystal eggs are exactly what they sound like: egg-shaped crystals. Some are amazingly made naturally, but more commonly they are artificially made into the shape of an egg. Crystal eggs are ideal for meditation and can be used in many spells that require the oval shape of power and abundance. They represent fruition in all endeavours and are particularly powerful when used in women's health spells.

Crystal Pyramids

It is not only archaeologists who study pyramids, but actual pyramidologists who conduct experiments on all sizes of pyramids. It has been found that if you place plants under a pyramid, they grow faster, or blunt razor blades become sharp again. Further, if you place your bed under a pyramid shape, not only will you need less sleep, but your sex drive may increase too. Combine this energy with that of a specific crystal and you have a double whammy of power to use in your magic.[2]

HOW TO USE CRYSTALS

There are many ways to use crystals, but here are the five main ways: elixirs, meditation, protection, visioning, and healing. Each crystal in this book will have some variant of these methods. However, crystals can ultimately be used in basically any magical work, and, yes, of course they look pretty.

Elixirs

Crystal elixirs have gained popularity in recent years with special water bottles that have built-in crystal holders; this

---

2. Learn more about pyramid power at https://aadl.org/node/197371.

is nothing more than an elixir as it's literally crystal water. To make a crystal elixir, place your chosen crystals in some water and refrigerate overnight. Always make sure the crystal is not toxic, as some crystals—not many, but a few—are highly toxic to humans. An example of a toxic crystal is vanadinite due to its high lead content.[3] Elixirs can be used on their own but also as an ingredient in something you are making, such as bath bombs, or in a recipe.

Water-based elixirs are the usual form of a crystal elixir; however, you can always use oil, vinegar, and alcohol. Cherry blossom and rose quartz gin is particularly nice! When making oil-based elixirs, only use olive oil as the base liquid as anything else will dilute the purity of the crystal. Place your chosen crystal in the oil for three hours, then remove and wash the crystal and leave to dry naturally in the air. Write on your crystal oil bottle what type of crystal oil it is, such as amethyst oil or quartz oil, and use as normal in your cookery and beauty products.

---

3. Review the gemstone toxicity table at https://www.gemsociety.org /article/gemstone-toxicity-table/.

If you intend to make water elixirs or drinking elixirs, always make sure to remove the crystals before drinking in case of choking (unless you have a special water bottle with its own crystal compartment).

Gem Sugar or Salt

Gem sugars or salts work similarly to elixirs and are an excellent way of cooking with the power of a specific crystal. The gem's energy mixes with the food, which is then taken internally.

Gem sugars are made exactly the same way as the elixirs, by placing the chosen crystal in the sugar itself and leaving either overnight or for a few hours depending on the crystal. The most common crystals to use for this are rose quartz, amethyst, and lapis lazuli; if using different stones, be sure to check their toxicity and porous levels. After the crystal has been in the sugar for a couple of hours, remove and wash, leave to dry naturally, and label the sugar with what gem was used.

Perform the same method for salt, though never leave any crystal in salt for a long time as salt is quite destructive and will start to break down the structure of the crystal. I usually leave my rose quartz or amethyst no more than three hours and then remove it from the salt and wash the stone immediately under warm running water, leaving it to dry on the draining board. Once again, always label what type of salt it is and use as usual for cooking, cleaning, cleansing, and consecration.

Meditation

Crystals are excellent when used in meditation directly and indirectly. The direct method is where you are physically holding the crystal to gain access to an altered state of consciousness. The indirect method is where you are surrounded by crystals with no physical contact with them.

Protection

This is probably one of the most common ways people use crystals as many will carry a crystal, such as an amethyst or quartz, in their bags or purses. Some will also have a piece of jewellery made of some crystal that offers protection.

However, the crystal does not have to be on your person to have the power of protection. A nice piece of turquoise or smoky quartz offers protection to both home and the car.

Visioning

Crystals are being used more and more as a visionary tool nowadays, though this is nothing new. Humans have always used crystals to see events of past, present, and future from not only crystal balls but also from black obsidian scrying bowls, not to mention obsidian mirrors and spirit quartz. Another ancient visionary method was dropping smaller pieces of crystals into a bowl of water and interpreting the shapes and patterns they created.

Healing

Healing is probably the way we identify with crystals the most as many people will use them for all manner of conditions, including the spiritual, physical, and mental. Crystals can help with every area of the human triad, or the mind, body, and soul that we are made up of. Healing elixirs are often used to great effect, as is physically putting crystals on your body where you have pain. For example, I suffer from migraines, and when they are particularly bad, I will place a lapis lazuli on my third eye to help ease the pain. The third eye is located between your eyebrows and slightly above your eyebrow line.

WHERE TO FIND CRYSTALS

The best crystals are the ones that find you. For example, while walking along the beach, there appears a beautiful piece of quartz. Crystals in their natural state are not the shiny, beautifully shaped ones you buy in the shops, but rather they are inside a piece of rock. The smoky quartz I find on beaches, for example, is encased in a white stone with beige veins running through it. The heart of the crystal needs to be polished, usually via a machine called a tumbler that grinds down the white stone, which is probably limestone or granite. The tumbler will then expose the full crystal inside and leave it looking smooth and polished.

There are other ways to find crystals; those that come to us as gifts from loved ones are also extremely powerful.

They come with not only their own unique powers, but also the energy and intention from the person who's gifting it, and if given in love, the crystal will resonate that feeling.

Crystals are gifts from the universe. They come from the sea, from deep in the ground, and from space. They are truly the embodiment of power and can create an energy unique to themselves and, when used in magical practice, also to you.

Always try to find crystals that have been ethically sourced or have been mined in an environmentally friendly way. There are three main issues when buying crystals: the working conditions of the miners, the environmental impact of that mining, and the carbon footprint that crystal has had in reaching you. Please try to buy from reputable crystal shops that will probably have notices on their websites regarding these issues.

Cleansing and Consecration

When you first get your crystal, always make sure to cleanse it. Simply wash your crystals by soaking them in some warm water, not hot, for about an hour. Then leave them to dry naturally in the air.

If your crystal is porous and cannot be immersed in water, such as rock salt, cleanse it by wafting it through incense. I have also cleansed crystals by rolling them in a dish of salt or sprinkling salt over them. All crystals, if in regular use, should be cleaned every so often.

After, and preferably on the night of a full moon, leave them in view of the moon to consecrate and charge. I usually say this to new crystals:

Welcome to my home, I'm making you my own.

In the morning, they are brand sparkling new with energy and power.

Some people also charge crystals by burying them in the ground and leaving them overnight to reenergise from the earth. Unfortunately, I cannot do this as foxes dig them up; they always know where the crystals are. So, if you have wildlife nearby, I would not recommend this way of charging and consecrating your crystals as wildlife can sense them and will take them home.

Storage

Many crystals can be on view all the time; however, there are some that require being stored away due to their frequencies, which can be very powerful. Always store crystals in containers made from natural materials, such as wood, cotton, linen, silk, or velvet (but be wary of velvet nowadays as it is usually made with synthetic fibres). Moreover, never store crystals in a plastic container as this can damage or disintegrate them, especially if your crystals are porous. Some crystals you buy will come with storage instructions, so always follow the guidelines for each semiprecious stone or gemstone you have.

Key Stones

In addition to the specific stones listed within each of the chapters, there are ten generic crystals many hedgewitches will generally have on hand. These stones can be used for absolutely everything and none are toxic, so they can be used in all manner of elixirs (except for rock salt as it can disintegrate when immersed in liquid for long periods of time).

AMBER

Keywords: Obstacles, luck
Availability: Common

Amber is one of those stones that has not only its own unique power, but also the energy of the original life force from which it grew—in this case, a tree. Amber is made from tree sap that has solidified over time and become fossilized. Amber is great for removing all manner of obstacles and enhancing love. Amber is also excellent for attracting good luck.

Amber Good Luck Spell

If you have had a run of bad luck, make some amber elixir and spray it over everything. On a Friday night, place a piece of amber in a bottle of water and leave it in the fridge overnight. In the morning, take out the stone and pour the water into a spray bottle. As you do, say this spell:

> *In all my ventures I seek good luck.*
> *Success can run amok.*
> *Whether health, wealth, career, or family,*
> *Amber, please bring good luck to me.*

This is your liquid luck; spray it anywhere and everywhere. Anytime you feel like your luck is getting a bit staid, spritz the amber elixir.

AMETHYST

Keyword: Strength
Availability: Very common

Amethyst is such a staple part of the crystal diet that if you had to choose just one stone to have, then this would be it. Amethyst is an aid to spiritual enlightenment and is also a lucky stone for lovers. It can indicate and aid a shift in consciousness and a life change. This stone can also ease stress and helps in meditation. It is the one crystal that is used for protection against the effects of alcohol and other addictive substances.

Amethyst Addiction Spell

Addiction is a disease; always seek medically trained professionals to help combat it. However, in addition, you can always call upon the amethyst and its unique power to help in that addiction. Write down on purple paper or in purple ink what you're addicted to, such as food, shopping, drink, drugs, sex, and so on. Hold the stone in your hands and cast this spell:

Trapped I have become, addicted am I.
Negative and toxic behaviour, why?
I seek the power and the strength,
To return to the positive and the light.
Help me in my fight, amethyst might.

Place the stone on top of the paper and leave it in view where your addiction takes hold, such as in the kitchen, the bedroom, the home office. Every time you feel yourself slipping, hold the amethyst in your right hand and place your left palm on the paper. The left signifies you are sending something away, while the right brings something to you.

CLEAR QUARTZ

Keyword: Success
Availability: Common

A major stone and probably one of the easiest to come by. Given its clear and undiluted presence, this stone is pure in power and can be used in absolutely everything. A good general all-rounder that can prove particularly powerful with money, health, and success.

Clear Quartz Success Spell

Write down what it is you want to be successful in, such as love, career, business, and so on. Hold your quartz in your right hand and waft it over the paper as you say this spell:

> *Success I seek in all I do,*
> *With everything I can view.*
> *Bring to me all I can see,*
> *Within the time of three.*

Carefully fold your quartz crystal inside the paper and hold it in both hands, close your eyes, and imagine what it will be like to have success in your chosen area. Imagine how you can influence the outcome, what you need to do, and how you will feel the successful result. The success will come in three days, three weeks, or three months.

JET

Keyword: Truth
Availability: Moderately common

Jet is often regarded as a stone of bad luck due to historical usage in funerary jewellery and is now associated with death, grief, and dying! However, it is an enormously powerful stone for revealing unfaithfulness. In the blackness of this stone, we can see the truth of the matter, and a piece of jet used in a legal situation will reveal the honest reality.

Jet Legal Truth Spell

If there is a legal dispute regarding anything from divorce, finance, miscarriage of justice, anything at all, and you are trying to prove your innocence while the other party is lying through their teeth, use a piece of jet to reveal the truth. The night before you are due to go to court, tribunal, or a meeting, perform this spell. Light a white candle and hold a small piece of jet in your hands. Into the flickering flame, say these words:

> *Bring into the light the truth of sight.*
> *Reveal the wrong for I am right.*

Say this spell three times and then take the jet with you every day to court. If things do not seem to be going your way, say the spell again in your head and imagine that candle flame illuminating the truth.

LAPIS LAZULI

Keyword: Communication
Availability: Moderately common

One of my personal favourite stones due to its healing energies, it is also extremely beautiful with its deep blue tones and golden veins. Lapis lazuli has been mined for thousands of years and was a popular stone in ancient Egypt. The ancient Egyptians used this crystal in all manners, from adorning temple walls to jewellery and headdresses, ritual purposes, and eye makeup (when ground into powder). Lapis lazuli is a wonderful stone for communication and is ideal to take with you when going for an interview or an audition.

Lapis Lazuli Audition Power

If you have an interview or audition coming up, light a blue candle and drop the lapis lazuli in a bowl or jug of water. Place both hands over the water and say,

Lapis Lazuli, help me shine.
I'm going to make this [audition/interview] mine.
Let me shine, let me shine, let me shine.

Leave the lapis lazuli in the water for three hours, then take it out. Fill your water bottle with the lapis lazuli water and take it with you to the audition or interview and sip slowly throughout the day. Good luck.

PEARL

Keywords: Beauty, success
Availability: Common

Pearls are often regarded by many hedgewitches as living organisms due to how they are made. They are not a traditional stone as they have not developed from the earth. They are made in the body of an oyster, a living being with its own energy, and therefore pearls have a unique power attached to them in addition to their crystal power. They have healing power and are ideal in transformation and success spells.

Pearl Mermaid Pretty Spell

In addition to its healing powers, the pearl is associated with enhancing beauty, and many glamour spells use them in some form. Glamouring is a form of magic in which the caster changes their appearance in some way. One of the elemental beings hedgewitches work with is the mermaid, who is renowned for beauty and beauty regimes. If you have a special occasion and want to literally shine, cast this spell as you get ready. Have a picture of a mermaid and a string of pearls, which you are going to wear. Place the pearls on the mermaid picture and say,

> *I call upon the sisters of the sea.*
> *Beauty and wonder for all to see.*
> *Show them how pretty I can be.*

As you put the pearl necklace on, imagine mermaid power pouring all over you in a watery wave of beauty. Wear the pearls all night and enjoy all the wonderful comments. After the evening is done, take the pearls off, place them back on the picture, and say thank you to your mermaid sisters for their beauty enhancements.

ROCK SALT

Keyword: Survival
Availability: Very common

Rock salt, sometimes known as halite, is a crystal that forms after the evaporation of sea or salt waters, such as salt lakes. Rock salt can form quite quickly, within a year sometimes, and is often mined and made into shapes such as salt lamps. I have a pyramid-shaped rock salt candleholder that comes in handy for meditation and transformation spells. Rock salt or halite is particularly good when used in survival spells, such as when you have had a setback or disappointment. It is also good in any spells to do with the heart and is extremely healing.

Rock Salt Disappointment Spell

If you have been let down by someone, make a water elixir with a piece of rock salt. Place your rock salt in some water for an hour and no more as it will start to disintegrate if left longer. Then pour the water into a spray bottle and spritz the water around you in a circle and say this spell:

I have been let down by those I know,
Disappointed and full of woe.
Salt of earth and fire of sea,
Bring happiness back to me.

If the disappointment happened at work, when no one is around, cast the spell and keep the water on your desk if possible, and occasionally spray where you work.

ROSE QUARTZ

Keyword: Love
Availability: Common

Rose quartz can be used in many areas from love and romance spells to helping mothers after a difficult birth; this stone is one of the great all-rounders. It is also good when used in an elixir, though even better when made in an alcohol elixir for family who may have been at odds with each other.

Rose Quartz Wine Spell

Drop a piece of rose quartz into a wine bottle then hold the bottle in both hands as you say this spell:

With this quartz I awake,
The family peace I must make.
I ask of you, fruit of the vine,
A family of love will be mine.

Leave the rose quartz in the wine for about an hour, then remove before serving. You can pour the powerful peace wine into a carafe and leave it on the table while the family eats and discusses the issues in a peaceful way. If the family is alcohol-free, use grape juice and cast the spell as before.

TIGER'S EYE

Keywords: Confidence, commitment
Availability: Common

Tiger's eye is often worn to promote self-confidence and awareness. It is also good for protection and is also a great stone for change, especially in love and relationships. If you have been in a relationship for a long time and now wish for a change or something more permanent, use this stone in a commitment spell.

Tiger's Eye Commitment Spell

If you've been with your partner for a long time but would like to get married, cast this spell on an evening of a new moon. Write out the name of your intended on a piece of paper and wrap a piece of tiger's eye inside. Then, holding the paper with the tiger's eye, say this spell:

> *Once starry-eyed and fancy-free,*
> *The one I need to marry me.*
> *We've been together forevermore,*
> *But now I yearn for something more.*
> *Tiger's Eye, I beseech,*
> *Let them ask of me.*
> *Let us be joined in loving matrimony.*

After, place the paper and tiger's eye in a secret place in the room you both use the most. Create a romantic night, wait three nights, and if they have not asked you, you ask them and see what their response is. Either way, your relationship will move forward.

TURQUOISE

Keyword: Protection
Availability: Common

Turquoise is said to protect the wearer from harm. It can also promote healing, friendship, and truthful communication. It can help you tune in to and understand other people, so it is a good one to have at work, not only for communication, but also in cases of backstabbing.

Turquoise Protection Invocation Spell

Awake the stone to protect in not only travelling, but in everything you do. Hold a piece of turquoise jewellery, such as a ring, bracelet, or cufflinks, in your hands and invoke the power inside the stone to protect you in everything by saying this spell:

> *Travelling from here to there,*
> *Wherever near or far.*
> *Protect me wherever I go,*
> *Backward and forward, to and fro.*

Imagine the turquoise protecting you on your commute, in your work, in the supermarket, everywhere. Imagine a turquoise shield of protection around you, and anything negative just bounces right off you. Always carry the turquoise on your person or in your purse or wallet.

The Quartz Zone

There are many different families of crystals with many relatives, such as jade, jasper, and agate, yet one of the most powerful is quartz. Quartz is the most common form of crystal and is the easiest to find. It deserves its own section as it is so versatile and can be used in all areas of magical practice.

Due to the many different types of quartz, a general description of its appearance is rather difficult to give. Further, quartz appears in many different types of rocks and is a very hard type of crystal. It is regarded as the second most abundant mineral in the earth's crust after feldspar.[4] Quartz

---

4. Learn more quartz facts at https://www.britannica.com/science/quartz.

is basically found everywhere in the world and in almost all rock environments.

Many of my summer holidays as a child were spent on the southwest coast of Ireland, where rose quartz was readily accessible on the beaches. In other parts of the United Kingdom, such as on the northeast coast, smoky quartz is readily available. There are more than twenty different types of quartz, and all have their own unique size, structure, and colour. They also all have their own unique energies and power.

CLEAR QUARTZ

Keywords: Spirituality, psychic awareness, memory
Availability: Common

Clear quartz is a transparent and colourless crystal and, depending on how it is cut and polished, can appear in many shapes. The common shape is the crystal ball, which appears like a solid piece of glass. It is due to quartz's spiritual and psychic attributes that it is often made into crystal balls or pendulums to help people see into the future and answer questions.

Clear quartz is ideal if you have trouble remembering things and is particularly good if you are studying for an exam and need a brilliant memory aid.

Clear Quartz Memory Spell

Hold the clear quartz in your hand and say,

> *Hear me now, little stone of crystal might.*
> *Memories come and go with the light.*
> *Help me remember what is wrong and right.*

Always keep the stone on your person, place it in your purse or pocket, and when you feel your memory fading, hold the quartz in your hand.

GATEWAY QUARTZ

Keyword: Barriers
Availability: Rare

If ever there was a crystal that epitomised the hedgewitch, the gateway quartz would be it. This crystal removes barriers in all forms, from a spiritual barrier to a physical barrier, such as overcoming a stubborn illness. The barrier is the hedge or border and blocks one side off from the other. In the case of health, it is the barrier between a cure and the disease.

The physical appearance of this quartz is also an indicator of its similarity to the hedgewitch as the stone will have an opening or aperture on the side that will lead to the inside. This portal is often regarded as an entrance into other dimensions and the other lands hedgewitches travel to. The colour of this crystal can vary.

Gateway Quartz Barrier Spell

If you are lucky enough to have a gateway quartz, try this barrier-breaking spell to travel to another realm. You can perform this spell at night and outdoors if you like, or you can try it from the safety of your sofa. Turn off all your lights and light a white candle. By the flickering light, hold the quartz in your hand and trace the crystal opening with your index finger to the centre. Say this spell as you do:

Remove the barriers of time and space,
Help me venture to that other place.
I seek the beings of my race,
The elemental being of fairy face.

Keep holding the gateway quartz, stroking the aperture. You may begin to see little sparks of light darting here and there or the candle may start to flicker. This is a sign you have been heard. Keep hold of the stone on your travels and remember to come back out of your deep meditation. Feel the stone in your hands and say,

I wish to return from whence I came.
I promise of this land I shall never name.
Return me now, one, two, three.
Gateway quartz, release now me.

When you do return, check the time as you may find you have missing hours. Keep your gateway quartz covered when not in use with a black velvet cloth and store out of reach of children and pets.

MANIFESTATION QUARTZ

Keywords: Dreams, ambition, promotion
Availability: Rare

A manifestation quartz has the appearance of a clear quartz but with one important difference. A manifestation quartz has a fully formed crystal inside it and is extremely rare. However, this is an absolute must of a stone as it brings about changes and the realization of dreams. It enhances everything within career, legal, and business areas, but it can also be useful in all areas of life where ambition and dreams prevail. This crystal always leads to a positive outcome; the only word of warning is to be careful what you wish for.

Manifestation Quartz Spell

Create a manifestation board or dream board with images of everything you want or like. Look through magazines for things you can see yourself doing or wearing or driving, cut them out, and stick them on your board. After, hold your manifestation quartz in your right hand and waft it over the images as you say this spell:

Manifesting with all my might.
Manifestation quartz, make it right.
What I see and want tonight,
Manifesting all in my sight.
I set in motion this manifestation.

Keep the board in a place where you will see it every day. If things have not started manifesting after a month, perform the spell again. Afterward, keep your manifestation quartz in full view on a shelf, altar, or table. Every day, make sure to touch it as you are keeping your manifestation alive.

METAMORPHOSIS QUARTZ

Keyword: Change
Availability: Moderately common

The metamorphosis quartz can appear clear, white, or slightly opaque in colour and is only naturally found in Brazil. This is a fantastic stone for bringing total change on not only the physical plane but also the spiritual and emotional—a true stone of psyche and soma. *Psyche* and *soma* are medical terms that mean "mind" and "body" and relate to how one interacts and influences the other and vice versa.

The metamorphosis quartz is regarded by some to have its own guardian angel or powerful elemental. It can help with those who are resisting change and heal the body by renewing cells.

Metamorphosis Quartz Transformation Spell

At times change is unavoidable, and though some of us thrive on this continual cycle of renewal, others have very real problems adapting to and accepting change. However, our world is constantly moving and evolving, and we need to be able to adapt, often quickly, to experiences around us. If you are having problems accepting change, invoke the spirit within the stone and ask for help. On a Sunday, cast this spell by lighting a white candle and holding the metamorphosis stone in your hands. Say these words:

> *Spirit of change, guardian of renewal.*
> *I know things must rearrange,*

But I ask of you, be gentle.
I accept all that must take place,
But please be kind with the pace.

After, look into the flame and meditate for a while, allowing the images of future outcomes to take shape in your mind.

PHANTOM QUARTZ

Keywords: Shadows release, ghosts
Availability: Moderately common

The physical appearance of phantom quartz is truly remarkable as it looks like there are two crystals instead of one. They are usually clear or white in appearance and come in many different sizes. The inner phantom quartz usually forms a pyramid shape inside its host crystal and is a real oddity. This makes the phantom quartz an incredibly powerful stone for all manner of magical practices, especially for a ghost investigation.

Phantom Quartz Ghost Investigation Spell

If you are going ghost hunting or have a presence in your house, use a phantom quartz to detect the spectre. Look through the quartz, including the phantom quartz inside, and scan the house or place. As you do, say these words:

> *Show yourself to me now,*
> *But do not scare me how.*
> *Show yourself through the stone,*
> *This haunting you shall not own.*

You are asking the ghost to appear through the quartz but also letting it know that you are in control. Always be careful when ghost hunting and make sure to protect yourself spiritually and physically. Always let people know where you are going and never go alone. I always say a group of at least four people is perfect for these occasions, and remember, do not bring any unwanted guests back with you.

ROSE QUARTZ

Keywords: Love, romance
Availability: Very common

There is no mistaking rose quartz; subtle baby pink hues radiate forth from this solid crystal. It can come in a variety of sizes and shapes from its natural form, which will be rather dull compared to the highly polished variety you find in many crystal shops. It is another crystal that can be found on beaches, especially on the southwest coast of Ireland. It is ideal for all manner of love and romance spells.

Rose Quartz Love and Affection Spell

A lovely little spell to use for some affection that can be performed anywhere, such as on a night out. Hold the stone in both hands, tightly clasped together, and say these words:

> *Little Rose Quartz of ultimate love power,*
> *Send me some loving this hour.*

Move your clasped hands to your heart, tap on your heart three times, and repeat the spell once more while tapping. After, keep the stone on your person until the spell has played out.

SMOKY QUARTZ

Keywords: Clarity, debt issues, pollution
Availability: Common

Smoky quartz is a crystal with a dark brown, grey, or even black smoky appearance, hence its name. There is a saying, *clear as mud,* which means there is something that is not easy to understand, as it is clouded by something. What you really need is a situation to be *crystal clear.* This is where a smoky quartz comes in handy, especially if there is a situation you just do not understand, and try as you might, the mud of incomprehension is getting thicker.

Smoky quartz can help with debt issues and is also good for cutting down the electromagnetic pollution buzzing around us. It can also help the healing process concerning blood illnesses.

Smoky Quartz Clear Clarity Spell

If there is a situation, a relationship, or an issue you just cannot seem to understand or get clarity about, perform this spell on a Friday night. Have a picture of the people involved in the situation or write down the issue on a piece of paper. Holding your smoky quartz in your right hand, say these words:

> *What's wrong with this picture?*
> *Quartz of power, come on and give me clarity.*
> *Visions clear through the quartz smoky.*

Waft the quartz over the words or picture and then hold the crystal to your third eye and close your eyes. Meditate on the situation and imagine the smoky quartz clearing the way through to understanding the issue. All the confusion and misunderstandings flow into the smoky quartz, making it appear darker.

SNOW QUARTZ

Keywords: Patience, perseverance, anti-chaos
Availability: Common

This quartz is best described by the other name it's often called, milky quartz, and that is precisely what it looks like. It is a pure white stone of snow or milky colour. As this stone's name implies, the snow quartz is ideal to use in weather spells and especially in ones that concern the winter weather. Some hedgewitches of the north will have a small piece of this stone in their car in case of inclement weather while driving. Further, this stone is quite good at combating the effects of a Mercury Retrograde, when everything seems to go wrong—mistakes in accounts, difficulties in communication and extra paperwork, files disappearing. This stone is sort of an anti-chaos stone and helps smooth out any situation that is getting out of control.

Snow Quartz Anti-Chaos Spell

If everything seems to be going wrong and there is total chaos appearing on the horizon, stop what you are doing and make a cup of tea using snow quartz water elixir. Place your snow quartz in a jug of water and leave in the fridge overnight. In the morning, make a cup of tea with the water, after you have removed the snow quartz and left it to dry. As you slowly sip your tea, while holding the snow quartz, say this spell:

> *Patience and perseverance, I invoke.*
> *Snow Quartz, I ask of thee,*
> *Stop the discord and bring harmony.*

Slowly sip the tea made with snow quartz elixir and let the calm patience wash over you. If the chaos is in the home, make sure to keep the snow quartz in view; if it is at work, take the quartz with you and leave it in view of your desk. Every time you feel overwhelmed by the chaos, make some snow quartz elixir and drink as needed.

Crystals of Earth

The crystals of element earth represent everything we find on our beautiful planet, from flora to fauna, to desert to wood and mountains, to weather and everything associated with its power. This is an area where we find all species represented, from wolf via the howlite to snakes via the agate. These crystals are the central element of life; they are the north point of a compass and will ground you in strength and fortitude. Further, given their power, which represents the north, they correspond to winter and its own set of correspondences.

• Earth Correspondences •

Colour: green
Season: winter
Direction: north
Governs: material world of possessions, work, values, morals, physical security, weather patterns

• Crystals and Spells •

The main crystals of the earth are bismuth, Connemara marble, desert rose, falcon's eye, moss agate, petrified wood, poppy jasper, snakeskin agate, thunder egg, and turquoise howlite.

BISMUTH

Keywords: Relief, stability
Availability: Rare

A piece of bismuth is a powerful gift from Mother Earth. This strange crystal is one of the first metals found and used in ancient times. It is usually sold in its many different stepped pyramid shapes, further adding extra power to it.

Bismuth has the healing power of acceptance with conditions and new treatments. The outcome is always positive where bismuth is concerned, no matter the issue or topic. Use in social gatherings, such as workplace activities or weddings, for success.

Bismuth Special Occasion Spell

If you have a wedding or special event coming up and it's been left to you to organise and prepare, do not panic. Instead, reach for a bismuth and start organising, safe in the knowledge that all will be well. Place your bismuth in your hands and whisper this spell into it:

> *Bismuth, pyramid of old,*
> *Let this party go well.*
> *Let all enjoy, Bismuth bold.*
> *Everything is going to be swell.*

Place the bismuth over your plans and every time you work on them, say the spell. Your party, event, or wedding will be all smooth sailing.

CONNEMARA MARBLE

Keywords: Remembrance, goodliness
Availability: Moderately common

Connemara marble comes from the Connemara mountains in the southwest of Ireland. It is a beautiful stone of green and is ideal for coming from the Emerald Isle. It is a stone that encapsulates saintliness and remembrance. It is also good for balancing all areas of life, including the triad of mind, body, and soul. Create an olive oil elixir with Connemara marble to connect with your ancestors.

Connemara Marble Ancestor Elixir

If you wish to communicate with your ancestors, drop a piece of Connemara marble in some olive oil and leave for an hour. After, remove the stone, light a green candle, and with your index finger, dab a drop or two of olive oil onto your third eye. As you gently rub your third eye with oil, say this spell:

Here in my third eye I contact you now.
The universe will surely allow.
Speak to me beyond the veil,
For I wish to know your tale.
Ancestor of mine,
Your knowledge divine,
Enter freely into my mind.

Close both your eyes and breathe deeply and slowly for a couple of minutes before opening your eyes, and stare into the candle flame. Then place your palm over your right eye, closing it first, leaving you with just your left eye open, and your third eye. Images will begin to flood into your mind, but concentrate on connecting with your ancestors. Many may come forward to connect with you. Stay as long you wish with your ancestors, and when you are finished, bid them farewell before removing your palm and opening your eye. Give thanks to the universe and blow out the candle; watch the rising smoke take your gratitude to the divine.

DESERT ROSE

Keywords: Health, wealth, surprises
Availability: Common

Caution: Unsuitable for elixirs; do not immerse in water or any liquid.

This is such a beautiful stone and is incredibly powerful for healing, especially with conditions concerning the prostate, testicles, and male reproductive organs. Simply leave in the bedroom and let it do its wonders. In addition, it helps develop psychic powers, and it can also bring pleasant surprises regarding unexpected money into the home.

Desert Rose Money Surprise

Place your desert rose in a special place and buy a lottery ticket. As you put your desert rose in its special place, say these words:

> *Make this place your own.*
> *Feel free to bring money into my home.*
> *Surprise me all you can.*
> *Desert Rose, I am your biggest fan.*

Keep the lottery ticket nearby and in full view, such as on the fridge door, and make sure to check it. Leave the desert rose to do its own thing.

FALCON'S EYE

Keywords: Journeys, travel, out-of-body experiences
Availability: Common

This is one of those stones that many hedgewitches will carry when they travel to the other realms as this crystal aids out-of-body experiences and meditation. On a physical level, it is also good for regulating cholesterol, easing throat conditions, and helping with travel sickness.

Falcon's Eye Travelling Spell

If you are going on a journey, whether physical or spiritual, carry a piece of falcon's eye with you. Before you embark on your journey, invoke the stone to help and protect you. Hold the stone in both your hands and say,

> *Travelling to places new and old.*
> *Familiar friends and lovers of old.*
> *With my Falcon's Eye, I am free,*

To travel anywhere safely.
Little stone of earth's might,
Protect me always when I travel day and night.

Every time you are going on a holiday or travelling by plane, train, bus, or boat, cast this spell to reinvoke the power of the falcon's eye.

MOSS AGATE

Keywords: Money, friendships
Availability: Common

Moss agate is an ideal stone to use when connecting with the earth to help your garden and houseplants grow healthily. Use the same way as a poppy jasper to make a garden elixir (see page 64). However, easing financial problems seems to be one of its main powers.

Moss Agate Money Problems Solve Spell

If you have mounting debt and few ways to solve money problems, a burst of moss agate in all areas of life can help. Make elixirs with olive oil for cooking, water for drinking, and vinegar elixir for cleaning. Drop your moss agate in a jar of olive oil for three hours before removing, then label and store as usual and use all the time in your cooking.

Place a piece of moss agate in some white vinegar for one hour only before removing and washing, then leave it to dry naturally. Add the vinegar elixir to a spray bottle and clean surfaces and windows and doors with it. Last, in a large bottle of water, drop the moss agate and leave overnight in the fridge. In the morning, remove the agate and use the water for absolutely everything—drinking, cooking, washing.

After, sit down with your moss agate products, hold the moss agate in your hands, and say,

> Spritzing here and spraying there,
> Moss Agate, you are everywhere.
> Send me the ways to solve money problems.
> Moss Agate, reveal your money power.
> Send my answers within the hour.

Use the moss agate products for one month, in which time the answers to your money problems will have revealed themselves. Always keep and store your moss agate with your bank information for extra help with money.

PETRIFIED WOOD

Keywords: Transformation, toxicity
Availability: Common

Petrified wood, like amber and pearl, is another one of those stones with not only its own energy, but also the energy of the being it grew from. In this case, the tree, which has become fossilised over millions of years to the extent that the wood has been replaced by a mineral like agate or quartz.

The process of petrification is turning something into stone. Many witches throughout history have been at the centre of this, and ancestors were often blamed for turning forests into stone. In Yorkshire in the United Kingdom, there was an incredibly famous hedgewitch named Mother Shipton (1488–1561); she lived alone in the woods, near a cave it is said she was born in and that also petrified people's belongings. Mother Shipton was highly respected as a prophetess as she predicted the defeat of the Spanish

Armada and the Great Fire of London in 1666, among other events. Mother Shipton's cave can still be visited today.[5]

Petrified wood is used in all manner of transformation spells and letting go of the past or of things that hurt us, such as toxic situations.

Petrified Wood Toxic Release Spell

If you have been involved in a toxic relationship or have memories from a toxic time in your life, use the power of petrified wood to let go. On a Wednesday, write down what it is that keeps haunting your memories, such as a name of someone toxic or what happened. Then sprinkle three drops of water onto the paper; as you do, say this spell:

> *Release me from the past.*
> *Toxic memories will not last.*
> *All the pain and the woe,*
> *Petrified Wood, make it go.*

---

5. Learn more about Mother Shipton's caves at http://mothershipton.co.uk/.

Place the petrified wood on top of the paper and imagine the memory turning to stone and becoming old and eventually forgotten. Leave the petrified wood and paper for at least a week before burying the paper in the ground.

POPPY JASPER

Keyword: Happiness
Availability: Less common

Poppy jasper is an unusual stone with red and yellow markings that resemble poppies. This crystal is firmly placed within nature and ideal for garden spells if you are seeking a wild meadow kind of garden. The poppy jasper brings happiness and energy and is said to overcome depression. It is one of the stones used to represent or heal the earth itself. In fact, this stone is often used in world peace spells.

Poppy Jasper Garden Elixir

If your garden is looking a little sad with wilting leaves and no flowers, make a jasper elixir. Drop a poppy jasper into a watering can and fill it up; leave overnight. In the morning, water the plants who are most in need of some happiness. As you do, say this spell:

Blessed little plants, do not be sad.
Drink up this magic water,
And you will be glad.

Use the poppy jasper spell every time your garden needs a little burst of happiness. This spell works well with houseplants too.

SNAKESKIN AGATE

Keywords: Friends, enemies, stamina
Availability: Moderately common

Snakeskin agate is a powerful stone and one that can come in either white or green, but it is unmistakeable with its snakeskin pattern. It is exceptionally good when used as a meditation stone, but also ideal when seeking out who is a true friend and who is really an enemy.

Snakeskin Agate Friend or Foe Spell

If you have a friend you suspect is rather two-faced and does not have your best interests at heart, try this spell. Get a picture of your alleged friend and place the snakeskin agate on top of the photo; if they are on your phone, stand the stone next to the camera. Say these words as you look at their face:

> *Are you friend or are you foe?*
> *I simply do not know.*
> *I ask of you to show your true self,*
> *So I can be sure within myself.*

Take the stone with you and keep it in view; within a couple of days or weeks, the alleged friend's true identity will be revealed.

THUNDER EGG

Keywords: Energy, power
Availability: Rare

A wonderful crystal to use in all manner of weather spells and one whose appearance is at first a bit misleading, as until this stone is split in two, the special inside characteristics cannot be seen. On the surface, this stone looks like a strange oval rock; the insides are highly patterned agate or jasper, probably with a deep cavity. The energy of this stone is endless and can be used in all manner of spells that require making the impossible, possible.

Thunder Egg Impossible Reality Energy Spell

If there is something you have been working on and everyone is telling you it is impossible, invoke the power and energy of a thunder egg. If you are unable to find one, print out a picture of a thunder egg. Write down on a small piece of paper what it is you are trying to accomplish and achieve. Light a green candle. Place one hand on the thunder egg and one on your paper and say,

> *Give me the power and the energy,*
> *To make this dream a reality.*
> *With all I have and all I do,*
> *That which is unavailable comes into view.*

Roll the paper into a little scroll and hold it in your right hand. Look into the flame and see your impossible dream become a reality. Meditate a while on how this can be achieved, then blow out your candle, watching the rising smoke take your request to the universe. Safely store your paper and egg where no one else can find them until your dream becomes a reality. When it does, dispose of the paper either by burning or burying it in the ground. Do not forget to say thank you to the universe for making your impossible dream a reality.

TURQUOISE HOWLITE

Keywords: Pets, animals
Availability: Common

I grew up calling this the wolf stone. It comes in two colours: white and turquoise blue, which can confusingly be called anything from white turquoise to white buffalo. It is great for creating a stress-free environment in the home or at work; it is also rather good for keeping wayward pets from wandering off too far, especially cats.

Howlite Pet Wanderer Spell

If you have a pet who likes to go missing for days on end, buy a little piece of howlite and have a hole drilled through it—jewellery shops will do this for a small price. Attach the howlite to their collar and cast this spell over it:

> *I seek you here, I seek you there.*
> *I've looked for you everywhere.*
> *No more the merry wanderer be.*
> *Stay in your own locality.*

The howlite will act like a beacon and bring kitty or doggy back when they have decided to go walk about.

OTHER EARTH CRYSTALS

There are many other earth crystals that can be used for the purposes mentioned here.

Alexandrite

A great stone for power and protection spells; in health, ideal for all conditions relating to the brain, including dementia, Alzheimer's, and Parkinson's.

Blizzard Stone

A good stone for all weather spells for all seasons, especially winter. In health, it is ideal for all symptoms of menopause.

Chrysoprase

Great little bright green stone ideal for all manner of skin complaints and for easing stomach ulcers. Also good when used for antipollution and can detoxify the area. Magically, it is ideal in all areas of fame, including with social media sites.

Edenite

A great stone for earth and garden magic but also for spiritual connections of higher elementals such as angels. In health, it can aid healing of the muscles, especially the heart.

Emerald

Emeralds were revered in ancient times, especially in ancient Egypt, where they were symbols of eternal life. These highly prized stones are ideal in conditions regarding the upper torso, so head, brain, heart, and lungs. Magically, emeralds are great in spells to do with work and renewing enthusiasm in a job you have been in for a considerable amount of time.

Feldspar

This crystal is often mistaken for quartz, but it is most certainly not. An ideal stone for finding your way and destiny spells. In health, it can aid healing concerning any effect from nature, such as seasonal affective disorder and skin cancer.

Fuchsite

An ideal stone for easing snoring and sleep problems; it is also great when used for maintaining healthy blood cells. Magically, I've used it for a whole range of spells, from money and finances to easing the pain of being betrayed by work colleagues.

Green Aventurine

An extremely popular stone and quite common in all manner of jewellery and statues. Ideal for promoting fertility and easing heart problems. Magically, it is great when used in spells for education and learning of all kinds.

Green Obsidian

Little brother to the great black obsidian, which has been used as a visionary tool for millennia. This little stone is ideal when dealing with drama-driven people who wish to involve you in their high-octane lives. It is also great as a protective shield against not only toxic people but also negative forces that wish harm upon you.

Jade

This crystal is still mined today in many areas of the world, including New Zealand, Canada, and China, with the biggest jade mines operating in Myanmar. Jade has been used and revered since ancient times, from China to Europe and South America. Its power resonates with easing a whole plethora of conditions from premenstrual syndrome to bone and joint disorders. A true healing stone.

Jasper

A huge family of different types of crystals all with their unique specific powers. A good piece of jasper is ideal for all spells concerned with family and relationships. In health, jasper is ideal for eye, ear, and throat conditions.

Malachite

An absolutely beautiful stone that is usually sliced in two, exposing its sensual patterns. A highly polished piece of malachite is ideal for boosting the immune system. Magically, it is used to connect with Our Lady Freya, along with amber. Malachite increases positivity and helps break negative patterns of behaviour.

Olivine

I really love this stone and use it for so many things. It is one of the most common forms of crystal and is ideal for helping with success of any kind. Magically, it gives a boost of success in all spells; in health, it is ideal for breathing problems, such as easing asthma and bronchitis.

Staurolite

The ultimate stone of connection with Fae and all those who reside within its elemental realms. In health, this stone can help with illnesses that indicate a loss of balance between the psyche and soma.

Tourmaline

Ideal as a wand and perfect for magical workings with animals who are frightened as it helps calm them and boost their confidence. Magically, this is a great stone for all manner of good luck spells, including increasing good fortune.

Verdite

This little stone can sometimes look like a piece of jade or aventurine, but make no mistake, it is a powerhouse of unique energies all on its own. Verdite is ideal for fertility and potency spells as it can help relieve sexual dysfunction. I have used it also to ease vertigo and dizziness due to problems with the inner ear.

Wavellite

A powerful stone for all earth magic and connecting with energies and elementals concerned with earth. In health, wavellite is ideal for helping people come to terms with a shock or trauma such as PTSD.

MYSTICAL BEINGS: TREE SPIRITS

There are many mystical beings who inhabit earth and frequent our plane of existence to not only help and heal but generally just for curiosity; fairies are the main ones who spring to mind, but there are other beings who live with us and are constantly watching over us. These ancient beings have been with us since the beginning of time and will be with us until we take our last breath. These beings are the trees.

In hedgewitchery, all life is sacred and magical, and the tree spirits are mystical beings who offer safety and stability and allow us to travel to other realms. As children, we are attracted to the trees, and as adults, we walk under them and through their forests to meditate and to heal.

It is said that every tree has a spirit, and every type of tree also belongs to a family of tree spirits, such as the birch family tree spirit, or the ash family, or the pine family. A specific genus of trees has specific spirits. When walking through the forest, woods, or city park, see if you can listen to their discussions, for trees like to talk and are very chatty. Connect with your tree spirit by invoking the energies of the tree agate and feel the presence of calm wherever you are. Carry a piece of tree agate with you as you venture through areas full of trees and see if you can hear them whispering to one another.

FEATURED STONE: TREE AGATE

Keyword: Family
Availability: Common

This unusual stone is ideal for strengthening family connections. It can also be used to enhance spiritual connections to nature, especially the tree spirits. Tree agate can treat pain in all areas of the body. It can also bring release to spiritual and emotional pain by helping one connect with the energies of trees.

Tree Agate Connection to Tree Power Spell

Holding your tree agate in your hands and by the light of a green candle, say these words:

I am hurting and I am in pain.
Let my aching mind, body, and soul refrain.
As I reach out to you seeking more,
Connect with me, dear tree spirit of yore.
Show me thy ways of endless peace.
Bring calm serenity, flowing now to me.

Meditate awhile, holding your stone and watching the flame. Imagine your pain and worries flooding into the agate, then safely extinguish the candle. Go for a walk among the trees and take the tree agate with you in your pocket. Breathe deeply as you walk among the trees and shelter under their branches. And begin to take notice of the trees and their sounds; occasionally touch one to connect with the tree spirit. Take your time as you venture deeper into the woods and forests and completely leave your worries behind. Emerge renewed and reinvigorated.

SUMMARY

The crystals of the earth represent that element which is our centre and our starting point. The north is the first direction we learn about, and if we are lost, we are told to find the true north and find our way home from there. The north, with all its power of material life and energy for change and abundance, can also seem at times cold and unfeeling. Yet the crystals that align with earth are some of the most beautiful and powerful within the correspondences of life the universe has to offer. If we are ever feeling lost on our journey through life, the crystals of the earth can guide us home and lead to our true north.

Crystals of Fire

The crystals of fire are as beautiful as they are powerful and all bring their own unique energy to this area, which governs action, passion, and creativity, among many other things. These stones represent the fundamental energy that created us—that power of an exploding star billions of years ago. It is that energy these crystals bring to our spells and magical practice. Through these spells, we shall make elixirs and oils and ingest that energy and power into our very hearts, for this is the area of movement and change.

• Fire Correspondences •

Colour: red

Season: spring

Direction: south

Governs: action, passion, creativity, enterprise, movement, positive change, love, sex, competitiveness

• Crystals and Spells •

The crystals of fire are blood agate, fire agate, fire opal, fulgurite, goldstone, heliodor, lava, orange aragonite, orange calcite, and vesuvianite.

BLOOD AGATE

Keywords: Protection, stamina, ingenuity

Availability: Common

This is one of the most important stones concerning protection and can shield the wearer from all negative energies. It is also good in the workplace for stamina and seeing through a project to the end as it can increase ingenuity within work. I prefer it for its powerful effects when charming a piece of jewellery as a protection shield.

Blood Agate Protection Shield Charm Spell

If you have a piece of jewellery you wear every day at work, school, or wherever you will be in contact with the person who is making your life difficult, charm it by saying this spell. Place a blood agate into a spray bottle of water and leave for at least twenty-four hours. If you can, gently wash your piece of jewellery under some running water, not too hot, and dry with a paper towel. Imagine the difficult person as you hold your jewellery in your left hand and spray the blood agate elixir with your right hand. Say these words as you do:

> *I bind you now,*
> *From myself and evermore.*
> *No more your negative comments,*
> *I charm this [bracelet/ring/necklace].*
> *This protection shield will now commence.*

Immediately wear the jewellery, and every so often, repeat the spell. Their comments should bounce right off you, and they will not upset you. Always try to rectify the situation by talking with them first as they may not be aware of their behaviour.

FIRE AGATE

Keywords: Action, integrity, motivation
Availability: Common

This is a beautiful stone of brownish red with streaks of cream and white through it. Fire agate is a powerful crystal when used to combat the hot flashes of menopause, especially at night, and it's also good for improving circulation. It is an ideal stone for improving motivation if there is a project you need to work on and just cannot get started for whatever reason. Fire agate is an excellent procrastination cure. In addition, it combats fatigue if working through the night to ensure completion of a project.

Fire Agate Night Motivation Spell

If there is a project you just have to finish and need motivation to get moving on it, try a fire agate elixir. In a bottle of water, drop a fire agate, then leave in the fridge overnight. In the morning, take out the agate and leave to dry on the side. When you start your project, put the fire agate next to you and work. Hold the bottle of water in your hand as you say,

> *Let's get moving, it's time for a change.*
> *This project will not remain the same.*
> *I drink this water through the night.*
> *I'm gonna make this project just right.*

Keep sipping the water all through the night as you work on your project. If you work the night shift, this water works well too.

FIRE OPAL

Keywords: Creativity, strength
Availability: Common

Opal is sometimes thought to be an unlucky stone, especially if it is in an engagement ring, and if using it in a crystal reading, it can indicate a possible death. However, this is an ideal stone for power at work and facing up to people. It gives its wearer added strength when dealing with a whole range of problems and is highly inspiring to creativity. It is said to induce daydreaming in the wearer; it also gives healing energy to broken hearts and restores harmony.

Fire Opal Creativity Spell

If you need to feel inspired and creative about something, try this spell. Have a selection of art resources such as paints, crayons, pencils, and pictures, or if there is a particular medium you create with, have it available as you cast this spell. Have an orange or red candle handy, but do not light it yet. Hold your fire agate in your hands as you say,

> Bring creativity to me.
> My heart needs to create.
> There is so much I wish to make.
> Little Opal of Fire, light the creativity.

As you say "light the creativity," light the candle and sit for a moment, watching the flame, allowing the creativity to flow. When you are ready, take up your pens and pencils or whatever creative medium you use and start creating.

FULGURITE

Keywords: Positivity, change, enterprise
Availability: Specialist crystal outlets

Fulgurite is made from the fire and power of lightning and is a gift from Thor, the Norse lightning god. The sheer amount of energy that has created this can be channelled into any project or creative enterprise and, as such, gives an instant shot of inspiration. Taken as a crystal elixir and used as a gargle, this stone can heal a sore throat; add a teaspoon of salt to the water to aid in healing.

Fulgurite Creative Enterprise Spell

Use your fulgurite to ignite a project with enthusiasm and inspiration. Have all your artistic resources, such as pens, paper, paints, clay, and so on next to you while performing this spell; the creative inspiration can suddenly strike like lightning, and you will want to start creating immediately.

Drop your fulgurite into a small spray bottle of water and leave for an hour. Hold the spray bottle in both your hands and say,

Instant fire into my project.
Inspire my [writing/art/task].
With this water, ignite the fire.
Let my creativity aim higher.
Inspire me, Fulgurite, inspire.

After an hour, remove the fulgurite and spritz around your art resources. Then spray the air where you work and walk through the falling mist of the crystal elixir.

GOLDSTONE

Keywords: Competitiveness, success
Availability: Common

Goldstone is the crystal of the gods; it has shiny pieces of copper throughout that sparkle like gold, and gold was always associated with the gods of old. It is a powerful stone, especially on Sunday, as this day is in harmony with it. It can help with circulation problems, including those concerning metabolism, and is also good with many stomach conditions. In a work environment, it is good for success in everything, especially promotions, but it is particularly beneficial in all areas concerning competitiveness.

Goldstone Competitiveness Spell

Cast this spell on a Sunday if there is a competition you are going in for or you've just bought a lottery ticket. Hold your goldstone in both your hands as you say,

> *Fire and ice, competition nice.*
> *I will, I win, everything I do is right.*
> *Goldstone power, grant me success tonight.*

Place five ice cubes in a glass and then place the goldstone in with them. Leave for three hours before removing the goldstone and leave to dry. Drink the melted ice water. Whatever competition you have gone in for, be sure to keep the goldstone on your person for at least twenty-four hours until the competition is over, and you have won.

HELIODOR

Keywords: Passion, balance
Availability: Common

A tremendous stone from the ancient past and one that is full of legend about gods and goddesses. It is an ideal stone for homelife and creating passion in both home and work as well as balance between the two. A good healing stone in all matters concerning the liver and kidneys.

Heliodor Work-Life Balance and Passion Spell

If life has become slanted toward all work and no play, rebalance that order with a work-life balance spell using heliodor. On a Friday night after a long week at work, place the heliodor in small jar of olive oil and leave an hour before removing. Run yourself a bath and place seven drops of the crystal olive oil in the water. As you soak in the water, say,

> *Passion in life, passion at home.*
> *Ignite enthusiasm for everything I own.*
> *Passion in work-life and in homelife.*
> *Passion and balance to end this strife.*

If you do not have a bath and use a shower, place seven drops in your shower gel bottle and use normally. Say the spell as before, and every time things get one-sided with too much work dominating your homelife or vice versa, perform the spell to rebalance your mind and soul.

LAVA

Keywords: Sex, fertility
Availability: Common

Lava is from volcanic rock and can be found in most places where there has been volcanic activity, such as Hawaii, Iceland, Italy, and Ireland, among many other places. It is healing physically and spiritually to the skin, as pumice stone is also made from this. Lava is also regarded as a female stone and is used in many sex spells, especially regarding fertility.

Lava Sex Spell

If sex has become dull, boring, and nonexistent in a relationship, cast this spell specifically on a Saturday due to its connection to Saturn, which symbolises negative feelings and limitations, but the lava stone will combat this with its fiery power. Place this lava stone in the bedroom and keep there for the entire duration. Before commencing the love act, hold the lava stone in both hands and say,

> *Fire, passion, and action.*
> *All that power exploding within me.*

Life's eternal energy moving through me.
Wills be done as two become one.

Keep the lava in the bedroom all the time, and when things start getting dull, repeat the spell.

ORANGE ARAGONITE

Keywords: Passion, success
Availability: Common

A powerful stone found in volcanic areas, such as hot springs and caves. Ideal for work success and competitiveness, especially if you and another company are networking and going after the same project or funding stream. Although generally this is a great stone to increase your success in any project, carry a piece around with you for relationships, friendships, and any work gatherings where you want to impress the boss with your abilities.

Orange Aragonite Beat the Odds Spell

If there is a business social evening and you want to catch the attention of the boss so they hire you for a particular job, cast this spell. Mix five teaspoons of olive oil with three drops of bergamot oil in a small dish or saucer, then place the orange aragonite in it and leave for an hour. Remove the aragonite, wash, and leave to dry. Get ready for your social event; before you leave the house, dab the crystal oil on your pulse points and say this spell:

> *See me shine, I can beat the odds.*
> *I am not a one-trick pony,*
> *So bet on me, and we will win,*
> *By the grace of the gods.*

Place the orange aragonite in your purse and carry it with you throughout the social gathering or networking party. Pour the remaining crystal elixir into a dark glass bottle and label and date it.

ORANGE CALCITE

Keywords: Love, sex
Availability: Common

A beautiful bright orange stone that looks like a sun and is said to increase happiness and warmth in any relationship, including love and marriage. In healing, it is also a good stone when treating the fatigue symptoms of myalgic encephalo-myelitis. Further, it can help with problem-solving and dealing with issues at work; simply keep one on your desk at all times to keep problems to a minimum.

Orange Calcite Love Problems Spell

If you have had problems in your relationships and need to address them but the other party is not playing ball and will not discuss the issues, create a neutral environment where you can both discuss the problems.

Create an orange calcite elixir by placing the crystal in a bottle of water overnight. In the morning, take out the calcite and leave to dry. Mix the water with some fresh orange juice and place in a jug with ice cubes and orange slices. Pour one glass for you and one for your partner and place the orange calcite on the table between you. Say this spell:

> *We haven't talked for some time.*
> *We need to address the problems that arise.*
> *I still love you more than ever,*
> *So let us deal with whatever.*

Together we are strong.
Together we can do no wrong.

Discuss your problems while slowly sipping the orange drink, no matter how long it takes, and work out your problems.

VESUVIANITE

Keywords: Motivation, action
Availability: Obtainable from specialist crystal suppliers

Vesuvianite was found within the lava blocks of Mount Vesuvius, and all the energy and power that formed this amazing crystal can be channelled to explosive effect. This stone can help with anger management issues and dissolves feelings of fear and restraint. This is an ideal stone to use in all areas of movement and action, whether for careers, relationships, friendships, or school projects.

Vesuvianite Moving Spell
If there is something you have been procrastinating about and just cannot seem to get motivated, try this spell. Place

a piece of vesuvianite in some olive oil for one hour only, then remove. Use the oil for cooking and moisturising your body. As you use this olive oil, cast this spell:

> *Let's get moving now.*
> *Let's get going with a pow.*
> *One, two, three.*
> *I am ready.*

Make sure to label the olive oil and date it; when you need motivating, cook with this or sprinkle it on your salad. You are ingesting the fire and passion of the vesuvianite.

OTHER FIRE CRYSTALS

There are many other fire crystals that can be used for the purposes mentioned here.

Aventurine

A brilliant stone for deflecting lightning in all its forms and for protection spells. Its healing benefits are ideal for lowering cholesterol and blood pressure. Aventurine comes in an array of different colours from blues to greens, oranges, reds, and silver. Aventurine in any form is a good general all-rounder stone for health issues. Magically, it is ideal in all areas of success.

Brown Topaz

Brown topaz is actually a reddish colour and is perfect for hip, leg, and knee problems. Make a gem elixir with olive oil and massage into the knee. In magic, brown topaz is good for positive change and passion.

Carnelian

A good stone for male energies and male fertility problems; it is also good for rheumatism and bone pain. In magic, it can be used in all areas of action and enterprise. Can also be used in many sex spells too. Carnelian is a good stone for those dealing with illnesses concerning a lack of energy, especially myalgic encephalomyelitis and fibromyalgia. Magically, this stone is ideal for self-empowerment and confidence-building spells.

Dragon Stone

This stone is often called septarian, but hedgewitches know it as dragon stone. A powerful crystal for contacting elementals, and not just those belonging to air and fire powers. In health, it is ideal for boosting the immune system and healing kidneys and muscles.

Honey Calcite

Although a relatively common stone, it can be difficult to locate a good piece of honey calcite. It's great at dealing with all problems concerning the skin and diabetes. It is good at spells regarding menopause and as an elixir or a gem oil.

Labradorite

An interesting stone that can be used for the majority of fire correspondences but particularly with enterprise and competitiveness. It is a fun fire crystal that can ignite spontaneity in any independent activity.

Mookaite

Mookaite is a rare form of opal and is predominately mined in Australia as many opals are. It has a unique power for enterprise and movement. In healing, it is ideal for reducing stress and stomach complaints.

Onyx

A great stone for calming nerves, social anxiety, and nervous exhaustion. Magically, this stone is ideal for success spells.

Red Jasper

Red jasper features in many tales of the Norse gods, especially the Viking and Germanic ones regarding magical swords. In healing, red jasper is good for all blood conditions and is ideal for those who work in the creative industries. Can be used in creative spells and magic.

Red Tiger's Eye

This crystal is good for protection and movement spells. It is a healing stone in all areas concerned with sex problems, especially with male libido. Use as a crystal elixir in both water and olive oil for immediate effect.

Sardonyx

A very unusual-looking stone with two or three layers of colours running through it. Ideal for all matters concerning enterprise and competitiveness; it makes the wearer's ideas unique and original.

Sunstone

A very powerful stone for all lower body ailments, such as stomach complaints. This stone is formed with lava. It is powerful for attracting prosperity and financial rewards.

Xanthite

This is a little sibling of vesuvianite, which is named after Mount Vesuvius. However, xanthite is found in the United States near New York, and although both are greenish in colour, they do have different properties. Xanthite is ideal in healing social anxiety and mental health. In magic, it is perfect for all spells involved in manifesting dreams and developing talent.

MYSTICAL BEING:
BRIGHID, THE FIRE GODDESS

The obvious mystical being of fire is a dragon; however, there is so much written about dragons and the element of fire that it becomes repetitive. There are so many stones connected to dragons or named after them, such as dragon stone, which resembles the pattern of a lizard.

However, in addition to dragons and the element of fire, there is the goddess Brighid. We may know her now as Saint Bridget, due to the amalgamation of Christianity with ancient Celtic beliefs, but her origin story is so much more fascinating, as Bridget began life as one of the magical beings of Ireland—a member of the Tuatha Dé Danann.

Brighid (pronounced *breed*) goes by many names, such as Brigit or Bride. However, all these refer to the one Brighid, whose name means "arrow of fire." She is one of our most important Celtic beings to call upon in all areas concerning inspiration, healing, and getting things done. Brighid is the ancient and ultimate Firestarter who can be called upon by simply lighting a candle when you need inspiration on a creative project or have writer's block.

FEATURED STONE: GARNET

Keywords: Energy, power, protection
Availability: Common

The beautiful red fiery garnet has so many qualities and can help heal all manner of ailments, including stress and pain. In the past, people often wore garnet rings or jewellery for protection, including from vampires and all manner of forces both ethereal and corporeal. However, its real power lies in initiating inspiration and action in people. It is a real motivating type of stone, so if you have a piece of jewellery with a garnet, wear it when completing tasks.

Garnet Brighid Ignite My Fire Spell

If there is a project you are working on or have not yet started or if you are at a crossroads with your creative life, call upon Brighid to ignite the flame of ambition and creativity. If you have a piece of jewellery with garnet, hold it in your hands as you say,

> *Lady of Ireland, Lady of Fire,*
> *I call upon you to inspire.*
> *Ignite the passion and fire,*
> *That which burns inside of me.*
> *Help me please to set it free.*

Put the jewellery on, light a red candle, and begin your creative activity. Always wear your jewellery when you are pursuing your creativity. If you do not have any garnet jewellery and instead have just a piece of garnet, perform the spell the same way and always make sure your garnet is in view of your art resources.

SUMMARY

The element of fire embodies those areas we all need at some point in our lives, such as action, passion, positive change, and creativity. The crystals we find here are ones of such beauty and mystery that if we look hard enough, we might just find a dancing flame of inspiration and passion within them. Fire is change and creation as well as power and force; fire crystals embody that energy, which we can channel into our everyday lives.

Crystals of Water

As children, we are pulled toward water; it is like a magnet to us. The seas, oceans, ponds, rivers, and streams all have an energy running through them that is both life-giving and, if treated recklessly and disrespectfully, life-taking. Yet this energy is neither malevolent nor benevolent—it simply is, like a shark in the water doing its own thing. It is not evil, it is just living, very similar to the correspondences water governs. These all have a duality: happy or sad, good or bad leadership. The area of water demands respect and acknowledgment of its unique power and energy.

The crystals we find within water are conduits of that power, and we can tap into their energy for both positive and negative reasons, but in hedgewitchery, we will concentrate on the positive.

• Water Correspondences •

Colour: blue
Season: summer
Direction: west
Governs: emotions, moods, fantasy, leadership, justice, career, health, expansion, marriage, peace

• Crystals and Spells •

The crystals of water are aqua aura, aquamarine, blue goldstone, blue jasper, blue quartz, chlorite phantom quartz, ocean jasper, soapstone, stone of Atlantis, and water agate.

AQUA AURA

Keywords: Expansion, possibility, marriage
Availability: Common

This is an ideal stone for stepping out of your comfort zone and expanding into new pastures. This crystal brings possibility in all areas of life, from relationships and marriage to business and financial affairs. A truly positive stone with all the power of the gold it is bonded with. Physically, this stone is good at healing all areas of the immune system, including genetic disorders.

Aqua Aura Anything Is Possible Spell

I really enjoy creating mood boards; they are not only good to look at for aesthetic reasons, but they are also perfect for manifesting realities. Decide what you would like to manifest, such as a new car, job, love, or house, and look for pictures that represent those things. Cut them out and stick them to a strong piece of card. After you have stuck all your pictures on the board, place an aqua aura photo in the centre and say these words:

> *Anything is possible when you put your mind to it.*
> *Everything is attainable when you get to it.*
> *There is no doubt, no negativity.*
> *I manifest it all, just wait and see.*

Place the mood board where you can see it every day, and when you get up in the morning, place your right palm on the picture of the aqua aura and say, "I awake you now; begin your magic today." Do this every morning until you start to see your manifestation becoming a reality.

AQUAMARINE

Keywords: Moods, temper tantrums
Availability: Common

An ideal crystal to have in the home if there are teenagers or those prone to outburst as this stone prevents quarrels and quells tantrums. It is named for the sea as its Latin name means "water of the sea"; aquamarine was a favourite in ancient Roman and Greek jewellery. Aquamarine also attracts good luck to the wearer or home, wherever it is kept. It is recommended to soak aquamarine in water overnight at least once a month to charge its energies, preferably on the night of a waning moon.

Aquamarine Mood Stabilizer Spell

There is nothing worse than walking into a room and sensing the negativity of an argument or one that is brewing. Create a room spritz with a piece of aquamarine. Place a piece of aquamarine in a spray bottle along with a table-spoon of salt, then shake up. Go from room to room and spritz the house as you say these words:

> *Temper tantrums abound,*
> *In every room, they are around.*
> *Spritzing here, spritzing there.*
> *Atmosphere clear everywhere.*

Walk around, spritzing and saying the spell. You do not need to say it in every room, just as long as it's been said three times. Repeat as needed and keep your room spray handy, leaving the aquamarine stone in the bottle permanently.

BLUE GOLDSTONE

Keywords: Leadership, expansion
Availability: Common

The blue goldstone is the aristocratic cousin to the very common goldstone of the brown variety. The blue goldstone can sometimes be mistaken for a lapis lazuli or lazulite given its deep indigo blue colour and golden shimmering flecks, but do not be fooled, as this is a crystal with an array of powers and unique energies. The blue goldstone is ideal in all areas concerning work, especially if there are leadership contests within a company. It is perfect for anyone who wishes to move up the ladder of success and can beat off the competition in one stroke.

Blue Goldstone Leadership Spell

If you have been working away, biding your time, perhaps as an intern or apprentice, but now feel it's time to step up to that leadership level, go for it. Hold a blue goldstone in your hands and say,

> *Up the ladder I want to scale.*
> *Biding my time like a snail.*
> *Ambition bursting inside of me.*
> *Leadership qualities burning free.*
> *All that power within me, now arise and show them all.*

Drop the stone in a bottle of water and leave overnight; pour the elixir into a water bottle and slowly sip throughout the day. Always carry the blue goldstone with you, especially during meetings, and begin putting yourself out there so the boss can see your potential. Perform this spell every weekend for a month, and drink the crystal elixir every day. Make a fresh batch every night after you come home from work.

BLUE JASPER

Keywords: Justice, inequality, career
Availability: Specialist crystal suppliers

This is the ultimate stone for justice and is often called the warrior stone because of its power to help those who do not have a voice due to inequality and prejudice. A great stone to help in all legal matters, especially where injustice is at the centre. Physically, this crystal can help with speech, sight, and mobility problems, especially if someone has PTSD or other stress-related issues.

Blue Jasper Justice Warrior Spell

If there is a cause you are passionate about and you want to speak up about something or someone who has been treated unfairly, perform this spell on a Thursday night.

Light a blue candle and write down your cause. Hold a piece of blue jasper in your hands and say,

I am strong, feel my might.
I am a warrior for justice right.
No more the meek and mild we,
For I have a voice and I will speak.
Warrior justice for the wronged.
Power and love to everyone.

Place the blue jasper on top of the name and visualise the moment that injustice comes into the light. Imagine a blue light of truth beaming out from the jasper, rectifying the situation as justice prevails.

BLUE QUARTZ

Keywords: Harmonizing, health
Availability: Common

A beautiful stone within the family of quartz and a crystal of infinite healing power. Use as a water elixir with sore throats for gargling and as a gem oil for massaging aching and painful joints. Emotionally, this stone is excellent for harmonizing a tense atmosphere and for those who store hurtful emotions thereby creating stress, which then leads to physical problems.

Blue Quartz Harmonizing Spell

The interaction between mind and body is psyche and soma. This means the mind influences the body and vice versa, and when we are stressed or worried, this can turn into a physical illness, such as a nervous stomach before an exam or being sick before public speaking. Blue quartz is an ideal elixir to make if this is the case. Place a piece of blue quartz in a little olive oil for three hours, then remove, wash the stone, and leave to dry naturally in the air. Pour the oil into a little glass spritz bottle and add three drops of lavender essential oil and three drops of basil oil. If you are allergic to lavender, use eucalyptus or rosemary as a substitute. Clasp the bottle in both hands and say,

> Stop the hurt and the stress.
> Psyche and soma, vice versa mess.
> Balance and harmony come to me.

In all I do, in all I say,
Harmonize this atmosphere every day.

Spray a few drops on your pulse points, such as on both wrists and just behind both ears, and massage in. Use this oil every time you are feeling anxious and worried about something. Always label and date your gem oils and be sure to use within a year.

CHLORITE PHANTOM QUARTZ

Keywords: Emotions, health
Availability: Speciality crystal suppliers

This is an amazing-looking crystal with a watery green clear quartz emerging out of another quartz, hence the name *phantom*. It is a wonderfully powerful stone for clearing unwanted emotional negative behaviours that are also self-destructive. Physically, it can also help with all problems concerning the liver, bladder, and kidneys and does a good job at getting rid of all toxins, whether emotional or physical. Use as a water elixir and sip throughout the day.

Chlorite Phantom Quartz Toxins Blast Spell

Make at least a litre of crystal elixir by putting a chlorite phantom into water and leave for at least three hours. After, take out the chlorite and leave to dry naturally. Use the water to make herbal tea of one teaspoon fennel seeds, one teaspoon cumin, and one teaspoon coriander seeds. Pour the boiled crystal water over the herbs and allow to brew for at least five to ten minutes, then strain and slowly sip the toxin blast tea while saying,

> *Toxins in, toxins out.*
> *Leave my body throughout.*
> *Toxins go and leave me clean.*
> *From the toxins I will wean.*

Drink the tea throughout the day for a total liver and bladder cleanse. Use for at least a month and see what happens. You could also stop coffee, alcohol, and junk food for a month and record how you feel throughout your journey to detox.

OCEAN JASPER

Keywords: Empaths, patience, peace
Availability: Common

A wonderful stone for all digestive disorders, including sea-sickness. This crystal is also ideal for regulating emotions concerning patience and stamina over a project or with other people, such as work colleagues who may test your patience daily. Magically, it is a great stone for empaths and regulates all their thoughts.

Ocean Jasper World Peace Spell

The ocean jasper is a beautiful stone to amplify energies of world peace. On a set day, such as World Earth Day, or on a full moon, use your ocean jasper to cast a world peace spell. Stand barefoot in the garden or on the earth, hold the jasper in your cupped hands, raise them to the sky, and say,

> *Holy, holy, holy, peace from on high.*
> *Earth and universe, energy of love apply.*

Healing of earth, sea, and sky.
Empathetic release, healers' sigh.
I call upon the powers of peace.

Touch the ground with the ocean jasper and say,

Heal this earth with ease,
Around the world with love and peace.

Reach out your arms and gently turn around three times in the garden before sitting down on the ground, holding the jasper to the earth. Imagine the power of the ocean jasper flowing through the earth and seas, healing everything with a glowing white energy. Remain seated for some time and meditate on the healing and peace of the earth. When you are ready to finish, say *thank you* and *so mote it be*, then get up and leave. Remember to cleanse your ocean jasper in water overnight to recharge it. In the morning, discard this water and leave your stone to dry naturally in the air.

SOAPSTONE

Keywords: Calm, soothing
Availability: Common

The power that lies within this stone is to heal emotions, especially sudden ones, like a panic attack or that immediate swelling of anxiety in social situations that many of us suffer with. If you do experience social anxiety in busy, crowded places, carry a piece of soapstone with you to help you spiritually and mentally rebalance your feelings. Physically, this stone can also help with skin problems, including those stemming from allergies.

Soapstone Rebalance Elixir Spell

If you are prone to panic attacks or are suffering from bouts of worry and angst, make an elixir with soapstone. Place the soapstone into a bottle of water and leave overnight. In the morning, remove the stone and pour the elixir into your bottle. You may add a few sprigs of fresh mint if you have any available, as mint is good for aiding confidence. Hold the bottle in both hands and say,

So many people both night and day,
Makes my heart and mind sway.
Panic rises with a fright.
Soapstone, squash that fear with might.

Take the water bottle with you and gently sip throughout the day. If you are prone to panic attacks, always seek medical attention first. In addition, make sure to replenish the soapstone elixir and have some on standby.

STONE OF ATLANTIS

Keywords: Fantasy, wonder, magic
Availability: Common

One of my favourite crystals of all time, the stone of Atlantis, otherwise known as larimar, is a powerful stone of fantasy and other worlds. It is a crystal that, as a hedgewitch, I use often to connect with other worlds, especially Atlantis and the vibrations of the people and beings located within. Physically, it is a perfect stone for healing all manner of stress-related symptoms, including a nervous stomach, and it can also aid in sleepless nights caused by worry and anxiety.

Stone of Atlantis Visualisation Spell

Visualise what it is you would like and place a piece of larimar in the bath. Add a generous scoop of Epsom salts and lie in the bath. Let your mind empty of all thoughts and worries of the day. Say,

> *I call upon the energies of Atlantis to set my mind free.*
> *I long to escape into fantasy.*
> *I dream of you and want to be.*
> *Let this moment last for eternity.*

Soak in the bath with the stone of Atlantis, and visualise the city and people; imagine all the wonderful sights and sounds. Feel at peace with all that energy, and when your bath is finished, remember to leave your stone of Atlantis to dry naturally after gently cleansing it under warm running water. Carry the crystal with you throughout your day and hold it in your hand when you need to remember the energies of Atlantis.

WATER AGATE

Keywords: Energy, moods
Availability: Specialist crystal suppliers

Water agate can also be called an enhydro, and it is the most amazing crystal I have seen; when you look into it deeply, you see the oceans swirling around. It has an outer casing of chalcedony, which holds the trapped water, and when you shake the stone, you can hear the water moving. Agate is said to give increased vitality and confidence, guiding the wearer with sudden bursts of energy. This is a good one to have for work if you suffer from the afternoon slump. If you were doing a psychic reading and agate somehow came up, or if the stone is chosen at random for divination, it often indicates a pleasant surprise for the questioner.

Water Agate Energy Jump Spell

If you suffer from the afternoon energy slump at the desk, pour a glass of water and add a slice of lemon to it. Have your water agate or a picture of it on your desk or wherever you are feeling tired. Start to shake your hands and say,

Shake, shake, shake.
Energy now awake.
No more the slump.
Arise with a jump.

Sip the lemon water throughout the rest of the day, and when it is empty, refill with a fresh lemon. Try this every day for a week, and your afternoon slumps may soon dissipate.

OTHER WATER CRYSTALS

There are many other water crystals that can be used for the purposes mentioned here.

Azurite

Azurite has been used the world over from ancient times. The ancient Egyptians used azurite powder to paint the eye of Horus in tombs. The ancient Chinese referred to it as the stone of heaven and used it to open celestial portals.

Blue Howlite

A wonderful stone for world peace and earth healing. Used for many spells from health to justice. Although it does look like a turquoise, its energies are completely different, and it is also ideal when connecting with celestial elementals, such as angels and spirit guides.

Blue Jade

A rarer form of the usual green jade, but just as powerful and ideal in all health and marriage spells. It was used in ancient times by healers as the ultimate healing stone and is still used today for the same purpose.

Blue Lace Agate

Scandinavian ancestors used blue lace agate in many rituals and practices to represent the Earth Mother. This stone is great in all spells to do with emotions and moods—a great mood balancer.

Blue Zircon

Blue zircon has been used for thousands of years as both a powerful ancestral stone as well as a crystal of peace. This stone can also be used in all areas of magic concerned with marriage and emotions.

Iolite

This crystal is sometimes called the water sapphire and is ideal for all balance issues, such as vertigo and migraine-associated vertigo. Magically, this stone is good for all areas concerning spirituality on its higher plane, such as connection with deities and angels.

Kinoite

A rather rare stone, but one that is excellent for connecting with the Mother Goddess, especially within the area of water correspondences. In health, it is ideal for fighting infections and viruses of any kind.

Kornerupine

Although this amazing stone can appear like an emerald, it is indeed rarer than its precious stone cousin. This crystal is ideal in all areas concerned with leadership and justice. Further, this stone is an ideal health resource in all areas of magic.

Lodestone

Magically a great stone as it has magnetic powers to pull anything toward you. In health, its gifts are to aid in healing with bone issues, especially arthritis and rheumatism.

Mother of Pearl

An ancient stone of wonder and motherhood, its legends stem from the South Seas and Pacific Ocean. It is a crystal for nurturing and soothing an active mind. A good calming stone for empaths, it makes an ideal present for those who worry for others too much.

Natrolite

A brilliant stone of peace, power, and leadership. An ideal crystal to have if embarking on a new career, especially if it concerns legal fights dealing with justice of human rights. It is also a good stone for overcoming obsessions or addictive moods and emotions.

Neptunite

A stone named for the Roman god of the sea, Neptune. This stone is ideal for all magic pertaining to the sea and its health. It is also good for use in spells to do with elemental magic and calling upon mermaids. This is a good stone for all areas to do with fantasy and moods.

Rainbow Haematite

A truly beautiful stone for healing, reducing stress, and banishing negativity. Use in all spells concerned with protection and hex-breaking.

Sodalite

A beautiful stone of blue that is ideal for balancing emotions and moods. Used in spells to do with peace. Physically, this stone can be used for menopausal symptoms, including insomnia.

MYSTICAL BEINGS: KELPIES

Within Celtic hedgewitchery, the myths and legends of water beings fill a huge part of any tale. It is not surprising, as within these legends I grew up with, every spring, lake, pond, river, or stream had a mystical being attached to it.

Yet perhaps ancestors were not that far removed from reality, as there is an energy within water. We are just learning now, or perhaps relearning, about the power of water. In the medieval past, waterwheels created power to turn the mill, and it is the transformation of energy that concerns us. There is a spirit in water, an energy that as hedgewitches we still believe in, and no matter the name we give it, the power within all forms of water is still there.

The water being known as the kelpie is a tricky creature as it is one of transformation and power. The kelpie for many is a water spirit that lives in Scottish rivers and lochs, and one of the most famous of these is Loch Ness, whose ancient creature is lovingly called Nessie. Kelpies appear on land as a horse, usually a big grey one, and there are many legends of unwary travellers getting on its back only to be dragged under the water when it returns to the rivers and lochs. However, so far as I know, Nessie has never injured anyone, although she may have startled some locals and lucky tourists who have caught a glimpse of her.

Nevertheless, the kelpie is a being who rides between the worlds, and it is for this reason that she becomes a hedgewitch's most powerful ally in the magical world.

FEATURED STONE: SCOTTISH SAPPHIRE

Keywords: Power, visualisation
Availability: Rare

Scottish sapphires are extremely rare, and where they can be found on the Outer Hebrides is a well-guarded secret. Yet these powerful stones have such a presence to them. I have a ring of Scottish sapphire that I wear when performing a visualisation journeying spell. Sapphire is a stone of truth and chastity and yet is also said to be lucky for lovers. It can also indicate peace and harmony, although it also has a power that will draw the past to catch up with you.

Scottish Sapphire Kelpie Visualisation Spell

This is a deep meditation spell that requires no interruptions, so make sure to turn off all phones, lock the doors, turn off all electrical appliances, and use candlelight. I find it best to perform this spell while sitting on the floor, so make yourself comfortable; put a cushion or blanket down. Have sea salt in a bowl, a blue candle, a bowl of water, a towel, and a picture of a water kelpie. Use a real Scottish sapphire if you can; if not, a blue jasper or a photo of a Scottish sapphire will do. Light the candle; sprinkle salt around and all over you and throw some over your left shoulder. Put your hands in the water and feel it run through your fingers. Say,

> *Calling forth the ancient energy,*
> *I seek you now, Water Kelpie.*
> *Enter freely in my domain,*
> *But take me with you when you leave.*

And for a while, let me remain,
In that other world of reality's refrain.

Dry your hands on the towel and make yourself comfortable; use the cushion if you wish to lie down. Hold the Scottish sapphire in your hands and close your eyes as you begin to relax, taking a few deep breaths and exhaling out.

SUMMARY

Water is such a powerful energy, and its crystals embody this. Water is symbolised by not only oceans and seas, but by all bodies of water, including us as human beings, who are made up of almost 60 percent water. As such, we can connect with those elemental beings and entities of water at a deep level. Water is our primary home, and who does not like to soak in the bath or immerse in a pool? The crystals we find in this area embody that energy and power, for water is healing, and water is life.

Crystals of Air

The crystals of air govern a wide range of areas from developing talent to communication, boosting confidence, and even hex-breaking. This is an area in which everything is out in the open air and there are no secrets whatsoever. The quickness of air spells to manifest that which is desired is also a wonder, as although no real time can be given on the outcome of spells, I often find spells cast upon the air are ones that come to fruition within days, weeks, or minutes even. Perhaps it is the speed of the wind or air that makes these spells appear quickly—regardless, they seem to manifest faster. Therefore, be careful what you cast for.

• Air Correspondences •

Colour: yellow

Season: autumn

Direction: east

Governs: ideas, communication, travel, technology, truth, struggle, beginnings, hex-breaking, developing talents, confidence

• Crystals and Spells •

The crystals of air are cloud agate, haematite, honey calcite, lodalite, peach aventurine, peach moonstone, silver leaf agate, tangerine quartz, yellow fluorite, and yellow jasper.

CLOUD AGATE

Keywords: Travel, hibernation
Availability: Rare

This is one of the rarer types of agates but still available to collect from a specialist crystal store. This is also one of the most powerful agates to use in spells related to healing after a long-term illness. It is one of those magical crystals that helps hide and cocoon you until you are healthy again to venture forth into the world, where it's a great protector while travelling.

Cloud Agate Travel Spell

If you are going on a long journey and you are anxious, the night you are due to depart, light a white candle and, holding the cloud agate in your hands, say these words:

> *Wherever I wander, wherever I fare,*
> *By land sea or air,*
> *Make my journey be fair.*

Look deep into the cloud agate and visualise the journey being perfect. If you cannot find a cloud agate, use a photo of it. Make sure to keep your cloud agate, real or photo, on your person as you travel.

HAEMATITE

Keywords: Technology, magnetic
Availability: Common

There is something so magical about haematite; it is a crystal, and yet it is magnetic, though it is made of iron oxide.

In ancient times, the Greeks believed if you scratched the stone, it would bleed, hence *haematite*, which means "blood." Suffice to say, physically, it can help with all conditions concerning the blood, especially the formation of red blood cells. Further, any concerns with blood at all, like fear of bleeding, haematite is said to ease. Magically, this stone is excellent with any problems concerning technology, but as it is magnetic, it can also be used in many spells where you wish to draw something to you, such as money or love.

Haematite Come to Me Spell

The magnetic power to draw things to you is phenomenal; whatever it is you wish to bring closer to you, use a haematite. Here is an example money spell, but you can do this with anything. Place your haematite on top of your bankbook and some notes of your currency and say,

> *Come to me,*
> *Three times three.*
> *I draw thee to me.*

If you want a love or career to come to you, get a picture of it or something that represents it, place the haematite on top, and say the words. Always keep the rhyme to three lines as three is a powerful magnetic number. If it is love or career or anything else that you do not want to multiply by three, change the middle line to "in time of three," thereby whatever it is you are casting for will come to you in "three time," such as three hours, three days, three weeks, and so on.

HONEY CALCITE

Keywords: Truth, communication, networking
Availability: Common

A great stone for all forms of communication, especially business communication where networking is involved. Carry a piece on you when attending social functions and gatherings for business. Physically, this is a wonderful general all-rounder of a stone that can help in all areas of health, including cell regeneration and detoxifying of liver and bladder. Magically, it is powerful in many areas concerned with spells that seek the truth through communication, including those concerned with social media.

Honey Calcite Social Media Truth Spell

Social media sites have become a double-edged sword in many ways. They are great pieces of entertainment, communication, and, at times, education. However, they are also incredibly addictive, untrustworthy, with a high level of corruption and deceit. Do not be tricked by what is written on social media by performing a truth spell. Using your phone or your usual method of accessing social media, open up your most frequented site. Carefully place the honey calcite on top of your device and say,

> *Whatever I do and whatever I say,*
> *Let truth forever venture forth this day.*
> *On the [social media site],*
> *Always let me know wrong from right.*

Visualise all lies and untruthful statements bouncing off your page and disappearing. If you use social media frequently, perform this spell at least once a week. Always use the honey calcite when you navigate your way through social media sites for the first time.

LODALITE

Keywords: Communication, struggle
Availability: Rare

An ideal stone for balancing life through all forms of communication. Lodalite is a member of the quartz family and as such has similar vibrations. However, lodalite can help in a range of other issues, especially struggles with their origins in the past and past-life problems. It is a wonderful stone for all magical practices and one that can have positive effects in all areas of your life.

Lodalite Problem Past-Life Origin Spell

In life, we can fall into the habit of repeating past events that may have been detrimental to us. We can relive the trauma of the past by our actions in the present. These could be from events in past lives, which we carry throughout our journey as we travel back and forth between the Summerlands and Earth. Summerlands is our place of transition, or heaven for some, but we are given the choice if we would like to return to Earth. The best way to try to find out about your past lives is to look through a world history book. Flip through the pages quickly until one jumps out; believe you me, they will. I have a deep connection to ancient Rome, the Anglo-Saxons, and World War I. You may also have encountered a very strong yearning for a place or country you have never been to; this is a remnant of the soul's past life and its longing to return home.

However, as well as the longing to return, we may also carry detrimental habits within us that are now affecting this present life, and we need to break those habits. Light some dragon's blood incense and one white candle and one black candle. Dragon's blood is the best form of protection for absolutely anything—always make sure you have some. Write out your bad habit or habits and place the lodalite on top of the words. Then say,

> *Negative emotions return to the past.*
> *Detrimental behaviours cannot last.*
> *In this life and in this time,*
> *I return you now, bad habit of mine.*

Meditate for a while and visualise your past lifetime and the habits returning. If you cannot locate a lodalite, a photo will suffice. After you have sent your negative habits back to the past life, safely extinguish the candles and wrap the lodalite or photo in the paper with your habits; keep for four months. If in that time they have not dissipated, perform the spell again.

PEACH AVENTURINE

Keywords: Confidence, communication
Availability: Common

This is a wonderful stone for boosting confidence, especially in those who are worried about their appearance. It is also ideal for those suffering with skin complaints, such as acne or psoriasis. Physically, it can help with chronic illnesses of the heart and lungs and aids in levelling out adrenal hormones. It can be used in all communication spells where the person needs to speak up and have their voice heard.

Peach Aventurine Communication Confidence Spell

If you find yourself always biting your lip and not saying the answer to a question in class or at work, use a piece of peach aventurine to help you roar. On a Wednesday evening, write down *roar* on a piece of paper. Hold your peach aventurine in your cupped hands and say this spell:

> *Hear me now, hear me now.*
> *I am [name],*
> *And this I vow,*
> *To speak up for now and evermore.*
> *My power to speak, hear me roar.*

Close your hands tightly, still holding the crystal, and look at the word *roar*. Think of all the ways you could have spoken up. Then close your eyes, open them again, and read the word. Do this three times, and each time, visualise the word *roar* in your mind's eye. After, wrap the peach aventurine in the paper with the word *roar* and leave it by your bed as you sleep. In the morning, take the crystal with you wherever you go and dispose of the paper. Pop the crystal in your purse or schoolbag—just always make sure it's on your person.

PEACH MOONSTONE

Keywords: Struggle, weight
Availability: Common

There is something very powerful about moonstones in general, but the peach moonstone is particularly potent for magical purposes. I have a set of moonstone runes, and about five of them are peach, and they hold such energy I love seeing them in a reading. Generally, all moonstones can help with women's health, including regulating hormones and fertility support. A great stone to use in all struggles, especially with weight problems. To harness its full power, always cast or use on a full moon.

Peach Moonstone Weight Loss Spell

Peach moonstone elixir can be an ideal hormone regulator and can help with weight gain, premenstrual bloating, or the dreaded menopausal pouch. On the night of a full moon, place a peach moonstone in a still mineral bottle of water and leave overnight. In the morning, say this spell as you slowly drink the water throughout the day. You can leave the peach moonstone in the bottle unless it presents a choking hazard. I have a sports water bottle and leave the crystal in while I drink the water.

From this moment until a month,
Weight loss, come to me.
Regulate all in harmony.
Find balance within my body,
And bring my weight back to healthy.

Replenish the peach moonstone elixir each night and be sure to drink it slowly throughout the following day for at least a month.

SILVER LEAF AGATE
Keywords: Hex-breaking, mental health
Availability: Common

One of the main powers of this crystal is the ability to limit or destroy a hex. At times in our lives, we may feel that someone has put a hex on us, in as much as everything starts going wrong, including phones breaking, TVs playing up, internet not working. These are all good indicators that something is not right, and the natural order or balance has been upset and needs to be rectified.

Further, silver leaf agate has many benefits and is often used for those with special needs, especially autism. This stone can help in all areas where mental health is concerned: sleep disturbances, migraines, and bipolar, among many other issues.

Silver Leaf Hex-Breaking Spell

At times, we can feel like nothing is going right for us and we feel like we may have been psychically attacked or hexed. If you know for certain who hexed you, perform this spell. Light a white candle and look into a mirror; have the candle to the left side of you. If you have a picture of them, place the silver leaf on top of their face and look into the mirror. Say these words:

> *No more your spiteful words.*
> *Your actions and deeds return to thee.*
> *You cannot hurt me.*

Return, return, return to thee.
Return, return, return.
Three times three.

Imagine all the things they have done to you and said about you returning to them. Imagine yourself as a mirror with the silver leaf amplifying the reflective quality surrounding you, creating a shield, and watch how negative words and actions just bounce back off you. After, always keep the silver leaf on your person, and when you are at work or wherever you feel most vulnerable, imagine putting on that mirror like a cloak, covering every part of you.

TANGERINE QUARTZ

Keywords: Developing talents, luck
Availability: Specialist crystal stores

A member of the quartz family and one that is so powerful for developing talents both known and hidden. It can also help to bring luck to you in all areas of your life, and not just that which is concerned with your talents. Talents can be anything and not just in the creative or artistic arts—a natural talent could be in learning languages quickly or reading tarot instinctively. A talent is anything you are good at, and we are all good at something. Physically, this stone is good for the effects of seasonal depression. Keep a piece visually available for you to see throughout the winter months in the room you most use.

Tangerine Quartz Good Luck Spell

We all can do with a bit of luck in probably every area of our lives from work to homelife, dreams, our talents, whatever it may be. Try to acquire a piece of tangerine quartz and keep it in pride of place in your home. Try different locations within your home, preferably the room you most frequent—kitchen, living room, bedroom, or even hall. When you are happy with where the crystal is, tap it three times and say,

> *Bring me luck in all I do, in all I say.*
> *But above all, bring me luck today.*

Every morning for a month, perform this little good luck spell and see what happens. If you cannot obtain a piece of tangerine quartz, create a small mood board from pictures of the crystal found in magazines or online. Hang the mood board in the room you most frequent and perform the spell as before.

YELLOW FLUORITE

Keywords: Beginnings, positivity
Availability: Common

A great stone for lowering cholesterol; keep in your water bottle and slowly sip throughout the day. It can also help with problems concerning the stomach and diet, especially if overweight, and can set you in the right frame of mind for a successful change to a healthy lifestyle. An ideal crystal when embarking on a new project or journey or anything new or beginning in your life—something you have never done before. This crystal brings a positive outlook on your new venture and the end result will always be pleasing.

Yellow Fluorite House Move Spell

A house move is one of the most stressful times in your life, but do not let the worry of moving interrupt your excitement for a new beginning. Instead, use a piece of yellow fluorite to lessen the effect of a house moving and its disruptions. Seven days before you are due to move, write a list of things you must pack and label. Place the yellow fluorite on top of the list overnight, and in the morning, begin to pack. On the third night before you are due to leave, look at the list again and tick everything you have completed off. Add some more things you need to pack and label, place the yellow fluorite on top of the list, and leave once more overnight. In the morning, pack the remaining things. On the day before you are due to leave, look at your list once more; tick everything you have completed off. Take your yellow fluorite and list and go from room to room; say these words as you do:

> *In this house I did roam.*
> *From room to room, this was my home.*
> *I empty it now of all bits and bobs.*
> *This move will be a perfect job.*

Wave your yellow fluorite slowly through each room like a magic wand, carefully checking that everything is packed and ready for the movers. Have a good night's sleep, and in the morning, keep the yellow fluorite in your pocket or wear it if it is a piece of jewellery.

YELLOW JASPER

Keywords: Ideas, confidence
Availability: Common

A beautiful little member of the jasper family and a good all-rounder for absolutely anything. A great stone for building confidence to express your ideas, especially at work or in a social setting. Physically, this is an ideal stone for dealing with stomach, bladder, and gallstone problems. Use as an elixir, but always check with medical professionals first, as larger gallstones will need to be removed by surgery.

Yellow Jasper Ideas Buzzing Spell

If you have lots of ideas buzzing around but you cannot seem to make them a reality, perform a yellow jasper spell to organise and discipline your ideas. Cut out pictures of bees buzzing or draw them. Each bee represents an idea that needs to find its path to the honeycomb, or fruition. As you draw each bee, say these words:

Ideas and thoughts, I have many.
All buzzing inside me aplenty.
Focus now and turn into honey,
Bringing me lots of love and money.
Whatever you bring, or whatever you'll be,
Buzzing thoughts, manifesting bee.

Meditate while holding your yellow jasper, and focus your mind on the ideas buzzing around in your head. Name each bee by writing on top of its picture the one-word idea (education, wardrobe, writing, poems, etc). Then place the yellow jasper on top of your drawing and every day, look at it, and view what is beginning to manifest. Find a little time each day, choosing one bee to focus on until they all come to fruition.

OTHER AIR CRYSTALS

There are many other air crystals that can be used for the purposes mentioned here.

Alabaster

Ancient Egyptians used alabaster in their funerary arrangements given its purity and durability and it is found in many tombs across Egypt. Use it in all areas of magic, especially when connecting with your spirit guides and animals.

Citrine

An extremely powerful crystal in all areas to do with business, enterprise, communication, and abundance and drawing positive things to you. An ideal stone for managing skin problems, such as acne and allergic reactions. Citrine comes in an array of colours, but the yellow stone is ideal for attracting prosperity spells and bringing extra energy to your magic.

Flint

An ideal stone for hex-breaking and dealing with negative people. A powerful stone that has been used for thousands of years by humans for building fires and arrows, tools, and so on. A stone of defence, protection, and survival. It is also perfect for helping with kidney stones, skin lesions, and skin tags.

Gold

Gold never diminishes in price and is a staple in all financial areas; invest in this if you can. Physically, it is an ideal resource to rid styes and other skin complaints, such as boils; rub the gold gently on the stye or cyst. Gold is also great for building confidence and developing talents, especially hidden ones.

Golden Labradorite

This beautiful little stone is ideal with all areas of travel and spells concerning journeys, whether the daily commute or spiritual journeys. It is also good for all illnesses concerning the bladder and gallbladder.

Graphite

The poor relation to diamond, this stone can help in areas of magic concerning quality and perfection. It is good for gut and bowel health, such as treating constipation.

Lemon Quartz

A great stone for balancing hormones and for those with fluctuating weight issues. It is also an ideal crystal for all areas concerning communication and struggles, especially with the truth and obtaining it from someone.

Morganite

An unusual stone that was named after its discoverer. A very powerful stone for amplifying all magical practices, especially rituals and invocations, but always be sure to protect yourself spiritually when working with morganite as it can attract negative entities.

Natrolite

When this piece of crystal is highly polished, it looks like a diamond and is actually rarer than a diamond. A powerful stone for all areas of increasing positivity, especially in communication and confidence.

Sunstone

A powerful stone of positivity and finding the truth about anything. It is one of those great all-rounder crystals that can help with anything and everything, including seasonal depression and building confidence.

Tourmaline

This crystal is good for cleansing and spells to repel negative energies and electromagnetic smog. In health, it is ideal for healing eye problems and throat concerns.

Unakite

A great stone for all marriage and relationship spells. In health, it can aid in nutritional and digestion problems, especially fussy eaters or those with nervous stomachs.

Verdite

This stone can often look like a jade or green aventurine, but it is certainly not. This stone has properties that can help with all areas of fertility and problems with sexual dysfunction. In magic, it is ideal in all spells related to the family and relationships of close friends who are like family.

Yellow Jade

A good stone to use while using social media and talking on phones. An ideal crystal with all areas of technology, especially when needing protection from negative souls who wish to do you harm.

Zircon

This crystal comes in a rainbow of colours from reds to yellows, greens, and blues. It is ideal for a whole range of magical practices from connecting to your ancestors to family and relationship spells. In health, it can help in conditions of the heart, brain, and mind, especially in mental health problems.

MYSTICAL BEINGS: AIR SPRITES

The mystical beings of air are as plentiful as cloud formations. Air rules clouds, winds, storms, and beings with wings, including griffins, Pegasus, and the sphinx. (Not all sphinxes have wings—ancient Egyptian sphinxes tend not to have wings, while ancient Persian, Sumerian, and Greek ones all have wings.) In ancient lore, any beings with wings represent spirit and messengers from the divine. One of the main tiny beings we immediately associate with wings is, of course, the Fae, or fairies. However, I would like to discuss their cousin, the sprite.

Air sprites are almost pixyish in their appearance and are considerably smaller than fairies. They can often appear as nothing more than sparks of light. Further, they are even more mischievous than their relatives, the fairies, who are positively mild in comparison. Despite their size, they have so much power and energy in everything they do. We can tap into their energy, but be careful with them, as they do tend to manifest in large numbers if openly invited.

FEATURED STONE: GOLD SHEEN OBSIDIAN

Keywords: Wealth, power
Availability: Specialist crystal suppliers

Black obsidian bowls and mirrors have been used since ancient times as resources and vehicles of scrying. Many shamans and prophets used obsidian; however, gold obsidian is often overlooked. Yet this is a powerful tool for connecting with a whole range of beings, from spirit guides to gods and goddesses to muses and to the sprites of air. The obsidian family of crystals is ideal for everything supernatural and wonderous about magical practice. Physically, this stone was often used to aid in genetic illnesses and is the go-to crystal of psychic surgery practitioners.

Gold Sheen Obsidian Air Sprites Power Spell

Always work with air sprites outside of the family home and do not invite them into the house, as they can be as problematic as termites. Place your gold sheen obsidian on the ground where you are standing barefoot. Then reach up, and then bend down to touch the ground with both hands, then stand back up as you say,

> *As above, so below.*
> *I call you now from where I do not know.*
> *Air Sprites, appear before my eyes.*
> *Let my powers rise.*

In all my magic from now until hours of twenty-four
Grant me powers more.
Air Sprites, I call you forth.

You may start to see little golden flashes of light darting here and there; these are the air sprites, and they can zoom quite quickly around. Go about your magical practice for the next twenty-four hours, but remember when it ends to give thanks to the air sprites for boosting your magic. I always like to hang ribbons or sparkly little objects on trees or tall bushes for them.

SUMMARY

The crystals of air are some of the most versatile; their power to transform energy from one source to another is astounding. It is for this reason that these powerful crystals relay the force that surrounds us all the time. This energy flows around us and through us like the air we breathe, an invisible strength only a small handful of us can see. Those flashes of light, that spark of electricity, the smell of energy in the air—these are all signs of that power and force. The crystals found in this section are not only beautiful, but they also embody that energy and power in a way we can tap into and utilise in our magical practice and daily lives.

Crystals of Spirit

The crystals of spirit represent the universe and all therein. The universe is spirit, it is the divine, it is where our gods and goddesses stem from. Spirit is the point of connection with every living being and energy throughout the universe, whether it is on this plane of existence or another. This energy manifests itself through everything, including us, and we can tap into that via dreams, meditation, intuition, and visions. Occasionally, the universe will send us a flash of inspiration or even a premonition as a warning, and we must always adhere to this. This area of spirit is where trusting your first instincts becomes paramount in everything you do. The crystals I have chosen will help you tap into those universal energies and help in your magical practice by enriching your spiritual contact with the divine.

• Spirit Correspondences •

Colour: white

Season: all

Direction: spirit / divine

Governs: spirituality, higher powers, interaction with all universal life, angels, aliens, psychic powers, intuition, dreams

• Crystals and Spells •

The crystals of spirit are angelite, angel aura, galaxite, meteorite Gibeon, moldavite, nebula stone, ruby star, spirit quartz, star crystal, star sapphire, and white howlite.

ANGELITE

Keywords: Higher power, messenger

Availability: Common

Angelite is a beautiful celestial blue colour and is an ideal stone to connect with your guardian angel. This little crystal can act as a protective shield while you are communicating with messengers from the higher realms. It is also an ideal stone for a great amount of healing, especially with thyroid problems and throat ailments. Make an elixir with it by dropping it into a bottle of mineral water and leaving overnight. In the morning, gargle with the angelite elixir.

Angelite Angel Invocation Spell

Call upon your angels and guardian spirits when you are in danger or facing a battle. Hold the angelite in your hands as you say,

> *I call upon you, Angel of Light.*
> *Help me in my fight.*
> *Under your wings, I am safe.*

You can use this spell anywhere and anytime you feel threatened or scared or like you are in danger.

ANGEL AURA

Keyword: Meditation
Availability: Common

Angel aura has a rainbow inside due to its pearly opalescence. A good all-rounder for healing and ideal when communicating with angels and the higher power, but also just as good when recalling and healing past lives and past-life trauma. Use when meditating to enhance the connection with the divine and higher powers.

Angel Aura Meditation Spell

Create a circle with salt, either inside your home or outside in the garden; make sure it is big enough for you to lie down in, and place a pillow in the circle along with incense and your angel aura. Light some patchouli incense and then sit within the circle, cross-legged to begin with, then raise your hands toward the heavens. Say,

> *I connect upon a higher plane.*
> *This world of darkness, for a moment I will refrain.*

Send me peace and tranquillity.
Safe and sound in my meditation sanctuary.

Make yourself comfortable and lie down in the circle. Place the angel aura on your stomach, just above your belly button, close your eyes, and meditate. Allow all the stress and strains of the day to disappear from your fingers and toes.

GALAXITE

Keywords: Protection, universe connection
Availability: Extremely rare

This amazing little crystal looks like a miniature galaxy. It is a dark green or grey colour that, when held toward a light source, shines with opalescent flecks that appear like planets and stars. It is just gorgeous and unusual but sadly very rare and difficult to obtain, which is a shame, because it is ideal for cleansing the aura and is a great protective stone as you are basically holding the power of the universe in your hands when using it. Physically, it can help expand mental horizons if you are suffering from a lack of support from service providers and experiencing mobility problems.

Galaxite Send Me Support Spell

Due to its rarity, use a photo of a galaxite and place a clear quartz over the photo to amplify the energy of the galaxite through the quartz. Sit for a while, imagining that energy seeping through to the quartz before you begin your spell. Imagine the power of the entire universe flowing through the quartz, helping you achieve your goal. Then light a white candle and say,

> *Galaxite of galaxy might,*
> *Send me strength and support,*
> *In all I do, make it right.*

After, visualise your goal coming into the light and becoming a success, then blow out the candle and watch the rising smoke taking your intentions up to the galaxy.

METEORITE GIBEON

Keywords: Unpredictability, excitement
Availability: Obtainable but rare

A wonderful piece of magnetic space rock. Just imagine all the energies and frequencies this little rock has experienced and interacted with as it hurtled to Earth. These frequencies left their imprints on this stone, and now we can tap into these. If you are lucky to get your hands on a piece, no matter how tiny, of meteorite Gibeon, feel its energy, close your eyes, and allow it to transport you through the beauty of space.

Meteorite Gibeon Ancestor Spell

As this is such a difficult rock to obtain, a photo will suffice. Have a photo of the universe and perhaps the names of your ancestors, if you know them. Look at the photos and names, then say this spell:

> *Through time and space,*
> *I feel connection to all the human race.*
> *My ancestors, I hear you now.*
> *Appear freely as the universe allows.*

Imagine soaring through space like the meteorite Gibeon, watching all the colours and exploding stars. As you pass a supernova, imagine your ancestors venturing out of this exploding star; see all their faces in among the bright beautiful colours against the blackness of space.

MOLDAVITE

Keywords: Otherworldly, extra-/innerterrestrial
Availability: Rare

Although this stone is rare, it still can be bought from specialist crystal shops; however, it is getting rarer. Moldavite is the result of a crashed meteor and is actually rarer than diamonds. If you do manage to get your hands on it, this amazing crystal is good for detoxifying the body of all the chemicals caused by pollution. It is also a good stone for boosting your confidence and destroying doubts. Ultimately, this stone is ideal for connecting with beings both inner- and extraterrestrial.

Moldavite Extraterrestrial Connection Spell

Listen to the sounds of a pulsar, which is the dead relics of exploding stars. The universe is so alive with sights and sounds, all trying to communicate with us. Hold the moldavite in your hands as you listen to the pulsar and say,

Sounds resonate at such a pace.
Swirling mass of fire flying through space.
I wish to connect with your race.

Although some people would find this a tarrying experience, we are part of a huge family within the universe; remember, all is connected. In hedgewitchery, every living being is an energy we can connect to, including those on different planets or within the inner dimensions of our own.

NEBULA STONE

Keyword: Beginnings
Availability: Extremely rare

Although incredibly rare, this stone is truly fascinating and is reminiscent of the night sky with its unusual shape formations and patterns. This stone is often called the birthstone of the cosmos and is made from a mixture of many different types of crystals, from zircon to calcite to jasper and many others. It is a great stone for healing the entire body and infusing energy and power into new beginnings and standing your ground on a project.

Nebula Stone Beginnings Spell

If there is something you believe in and want to get started but you need to stand your ground as no one else believes in you, use the nebula stone to begin your project. Say,

> *Here I stand with stone in hand.*
> *I cast and I create.*
> *This project I will make.*
> *All the success I can see,*
> *Just you all wait and see.*
> *I begin my project, one, two, three.*

Start your project, and whenever someone utters negative remarks or does not believe in you, recast the spell. As an added *oomph* to your spell, put the picture of the universe up or keep the nebula stone on your desk.

RUBY STAR

Keywords: Perfectionist, love
Availability: Rare

A truly beautiful ruby with an amazing star inside—a rare prize indeed, and with remarkable properties. Ruby is said to increase energy, support friendships, and aid intuition. It also fosters romance, marriage, integrity, devotion, and passion. Its positive energy helps in all matters of love and can increase virility. The holder of this stone can become a perfectionist with a taste for the finer things in life. It is also a powerful stone for amplifying magical powers through dreams and intuition.

Ruby Star Dream Manifestation Spell

See the truth in dreams and manifest their power into reality to answer questions and make decisions. Before you go to bed, meditate on the picture of a ruby star and ask your question, then say,

> Little star here in my hand,
> Cast your power of my mind.
> Let me dream of all I can.
> Bring forth the dream into my time,
> Manifesting all that I am.

Have your notebook handy and immediately upon waking in the morning, write down what you have seen, experienced, and dreamed. Remember your dream throughout the day as subtle signs may come to you regarding the answer to your question.

SPIRIT QUARTZ

Keywords: Paranormal, self-acceptance
Availability: Moderately rare

This is often called a cactus quartz given its appearance, but it is incredibly good at connecting with spirit. It is a quartz with little crystals growing on it and is quite beautiful to look at. This stone helps in all matters relating to skin conditions, from scars to melanomas to acne; spiritually, it can help with feelings of loneliness and being different.

Spirit Quartz Self-Acceptance Spell

If you are having problems accepting your differences every day, use a mirror and a spirit quartz to align your spirituality with your physicality. Look into the mirror while holding your spirit quartz or a photo of it and say into your reflection,

I accept my individuality.
I am unique and pretty.

In all I do, in all I say,
I am different and beautiful in every way.

Repeat this spell every day for nine days until you feel balanced and at ease with yourself. If at any time you feel your confidence waning, recast the spell.

STAR CRYSTAL

Keywords: Psychic awareness, intuition
Availability: Rare

Star crystal is otherwise known as muscovite and was once used for window glass. However, it is now just sold in the usual pieces, such as in jewellery and various wands. It is a perfect stone for connecting with your spirituality and heightening your psychic awareness. It amplifies your psychic abilities and is also good as a good luck charm or talisman.

Star Crystal Psychic Awareness Spell

Increase your psychic awareness by casting a spell using a piece of muscovite or star crystal. Have a notepad and pen next to you and hold a piece of muscovite in the palm of your hands. Cast this spell:

Beaming out across the sky,
Hear me loud and clear,
Spirits of past, present, and future come near.
Let me see beyond the planes,
All there is behind the panes.

Meditate for a while on the images that fill your head and write down what you see. Train your mind to see the signs connected to work, home, school, or relationships. And if you are feeling lucky, go buy a lottery ticket.

STAR SAPPHIRE

Keywords: Confidence, mediumship
Availability: Rare

An incredibly rare crystal but also so beautiful with a star at each end or running through it when it is cut and sliced. A powerful stone that enhances mediumship skills and connection to the divine. This crystal enhances confidence in people who have been put down all their lives by others who wished to control them and were negative about their abilities. This stone increases the power to succeed when you have overcome the naysayers.

Star Sapphire, I Will Show You Spell

Whatever it is you want to do that other people have told you isn't possible, find a picture that represents it—a graduation, awards, money, a big house. Cut it out and place both your hands and the sapphire on it. Imagine yourself in the picture receiving the awards, living in the house … When you are ready, say these words:

> *Watch me now, watch me grow.*
> *I will show you how, look at me go.*

Meditate on the picture for a while then carefully roll it up and tie it with a little white ribbon. Keep it safe somewhere out of sight from others who may ridicule your ambitions and dreams.

WHITE HOWLITE

Keywords: Sleep, dreams
Availability: Common

White howlite specifically is good for sleep problems including insomnia and sleep apnoea. It is also good for all success and education spells, but then again, a good night's sleep is beneficial for so many things when we need to be at our optimum level.

White Howlite Sleepy Dreamer Spell

White howlite is the best crystal to use for enhancing a good night's sleep and for creating a wonderful dreamworld you can slip into. If you want to remember your dreams first thing when you wake up, make sure to have a notepad and pen near your bed. Then before you go to sleep, hold the white howlite in both hands and say,

> *Mighty little Howlite,*
> *Send me sleep and dreams tonight.*
> *Encase me with pure white light.*
> *Safe and sound, dreams abound.*

Slip the howlite under your pillow and sleep well. Let go of all day-to-day problems and concerns and instead visualise your favourite dreamworld of magic. Imagine yourself diving into a different world and fall asleep in your magical dream. In the morning when you wake, write down your amazing dreams first thing as there may be messengers from spirit in them.

Your white howlite will need to be charged once every full moon cycle, so every four weeks or so, leave it out on a window ledge for the full moon to charge it overnight.

OTHER SPIRIT CRYSTALS

Here are several crystals that can be used in place of the ones mentioned; these are considerably easier to acquire via a crystal store or online.

Clear Calcite

Calcite crystals are a huge family with three hundred recorded different types. The clear calcite is a great all-rounder crystal in all manner of higher power magic and intuition spells.

Clear Fluorite

A great crystal for everything within this area of the pentagram as it is ideal for all matters concerning spirit work and communication with the other side.

Clear Topaz

Good old topaz is perfect for spells involving manifestation and love. In healing, this stone is said to increase the speed of recovery and can also help in the area of the lungs, especially where it concerns bronchitis and allergies.

Diamond

Diamonds are quite common and, surprisingly, you can pick them up quite cheaply online for all manner of spells and magical practices. Extremely useful in dreamwork and transformation spells.

Mica

This stone has been used across the ancient world from the Egyptians to the Aztecs. It has so many wonderful magical properties that can be used for almost anything, including contacting ancestors and protection spells. In health, it is ideal for alleviating the effects of dehydration and improving memory.

Milky Opal

Opals are a wonderful stone and cover a whole range of magical work. Use for anything, especially invocations and working with deities.

Norwegian Moonstone

This crystal also goes by the name of larvikite, after the small town in Norway where it is mined. It is an excellent stone for fulfilling dreams and ambition spells. In health, it can help with hormonal changes, including premenstrual syndrome, menopause, and diabetes.

Oligoclase

This lovely white stone is often mistaken for its sister the moonstone, and it can be used for the same things. In addition, it can be used for connection with ancestors and ghosts.

Prehnite

A stone of power to contact ancestors and engage in past-life regression magic. In health, it is said to alleviate fatigue.

Satin Spar

This amazing-looking crystal is a wonderful wand to use for all manner of spell work and healing the spirit.

White Celestite

A perfect stone to enhance psychic awareness and communication with all beings throughout the universe.

White Moonstone

An ideal crystal for psychic awareness, ghost hunting, and the paranormal. As a healing stone, it can help in all areas of women's health and is also good at healing childhood illnesses, such as measles and chickenpox.

White Selenite

A beautiful-looking stone that is ideal as a substitute for a nebula stone and is named after the moon goddess Selene. This lovely stone glows in the moonlight.

MYSTICAL BEINGS: THE ANCIENTS

The area of mystical beings in spirit is endless as all manner of both supernatural and paranormal entities exist here, from ghosts and poltergeists to angels and space brethren near and far. As a hedgewitch, this is an area where every possibility can be explored and experienced if you are brave enough.

There is a set of energies within spirit that is regarded as the ancients. These entities as they are now have neither been angels nor gods but may have walked the earth in human form at one time. In Celtic myth and legend, there are quite a few of them in ancient texts about the classical and medieval lives of our ancestors. One is Merlin.

The character of Merlin first appears in the medieval tale of the twelfth century by Geoffrey of Monmouth.[6] Merlin is the wizard of King Arthur among other things, but he represents the magic and power of the ancients. It is no surprise that the stone named after him is the ultimate stone of magic.

6. Joshua J. Mark, "Merlin," World History Encyclopedia, April 24, 2019, https://www.worldhistory.org/Merlin/.

FEATURED STONE: MERLINITE

Keywords: Alchemy, magic, wizard
Availability: Rare

This little stone is highly prized among practitioners of the Craft as it enhances magical knowledge. It is a small white stone with black inclusions, and if found in a round form it is said to represent the Goddess herself. As a healing crystal, its power lies in helping the body remove blockages to enhance psychic development. A deeply powerful stone for all those who work within magic but particularly useful to those who are new to the Craft and are still learning.

Merlinite Invitation to Merlin Spell

This spell is best performed outdoors in a garden space; however, if this is not possible, indoors will suffice. Create a circle of salt, for although you are inviting Merlin into your life, you do not want him roaming around. Plus, as you leave the door open in this spell, we do not want anything else joining him.

For the spell, you will need a white candle, Merlinite, a little bowl of salt, and a mirror. Make sure all are in the circle before you begin. Light the candle and hold the Merlinite in your hands and say,

> *Merlin, I reach out to you now.*
> *Guide me in magic for I don't know how.*
> *I am new to this craft,*
> *But help me make my magic last.*
> *I open the door and leave for you.*
> *Enter freely, now come into view.*

Look into the mirror and watch the images form, close your eyes, and open them; do this three times, and then look into the mirror again. Hold the mirror to look over your shoulder and scan the area around you. You may see flashes of light, or images of past times, or Merlin himself.

After you have finished communing with Merlin, close the circle and cleanse the Merlinite by rolling it in the bowl of salt. As you do, say these words:

> *Thank you for speaking with me.*
> *Merlin, thank you for your grace.*

But now the circle is closing,
And now we must return to our fate.
I cleanse the stone and close the gate.

Hold the mirror as before and scan the area. Make sure nothing has found its way out before you close the circle.

SUMMARY

Spirit is an area that is both huge and endless. It is an eternity wrapped inside the ultimate power of all, including ancients, spirits, and ghosts, along with angels and every part of the paranormal. The crystals of spirit are powerful in their own right as they can heal and guide, but combined with the energies of the universe, they extend their force and strength to unimaginable possibilities.

Crystal Divination

Crystals are often used in divination and there are many methods of practice. Here is the one that I prefer. It uses twenty-five stones, and when we apply the methods of numerology, this number condenses to the magical seven.[7] However, although I list twenty-five stones, these are only recommendations as you may have crystals that mean a lot to you specifically or it may be too difficult to attain some of these stones. In these cases, it is fine to substitute one type of crystal for another, but always do your individual research on that chosen crystal.

---

7. For an explanation on the number seven, please see *The Hedgewitch's Little Book of Flower Spells* (Llewellyn Publications, 2023).

GATHERING AND USING THE STONES

There are a few ways you could develop your divination stones; one is buying a complete set specifically for divination. There are many manufacturers of these, and several crystal shops will sell these ready-made sets. The other way, which is slightly more fun, is to grow and develop your own set by buying individual stones from various places. The crystals need to be tumbled stones of no more than an inch in length—a good medium size you can hold in the palm of your hand. The stones you will need are amethyst, aquamarine, beryl, bloodstone, clear quartz, diamond, emerald, fossil agate, green jasper, iron pyrite, jade, jet, labradorite, moonstone, opal, pink jasper, red jasper, rose quartz, ruby, sapphire, sardonyx, tektite, tiger's eye, topaz, and turquoise.

When you get your stones home, make sure to cleanse and consecrate them as normal. Always keep your divination crystals in a cloth, preferably velvet, bag, and keep separate from the other stones you would use in your daily magical practice. The divination crystals have one purpose and one purpose only, and that is to see future or past events, answer questions in the present, and give guidance in areas of much-needed help.

Getting Started

Light a candle and take a couple of deep breaths to relax, then focus your mind on a question or query you have and begin to pull out crystals from the bag. I always keep my eyes closed as this helps focus my question. Pull five crystals: the first stone as the past, the second stone as the present situation, the third stone as the issues surrounding the present, the fourth stone as the future, and the final stone as the outcome of your reading.

CRYSTALS AND MEANINGS

Crystals, unlike some other forms of divination, always give it to you straight; there is no mystery or wondering about a particular situation with crystals. The answer to any question will always be a clear yes or no, and no matter how many times you pull them from the bag, the answer will always be the same. Enjoy!

Amethyst

Although a generally positive crystal and an ideal one for lovers, this stone can also be rather negative. In a reading, it can indicate something of value may be lost, including love, career, and relationships. However, it is a yes stone to any question.

Aquamarine

A wonderful stone for all manner of reasons, but in a reading, it can indicate someone who does not believe in anything and is sceptical of everything. However, it can also mean success in exams and study and is a definitive yes answer to any question.

Beryl

A pretty little stone and one that can indicate a number of things in a reading, especially concerning psychic abilities. It can indicate that the person is becoming enlightened and their abilities are growing.

Bloodstone

This stone is often an indicator that someone is suffering from stress. It can also indicate an unpleasant surprise. In a question, it represents a negative answer and is definitely a no.

Clear Quartz

The ultimate crystal in divination and it signifies a return to good health and vitality. It is a positive sign in any reading and means a firm yes to the question. It can also indicate someone who has psychic abilities but also says they should take on more responsibility and stop relying on others as much.

Diamond

The most expensive crystal, this precious stone is also very hard and is used in drill bits because it is so strong. In a reading, it is an extremely positive stone and indicates a business promotion. In a question, it is a resounding yes.

Emerald

A beautiful positive stone that in a reading can indicate a secret admirer in the questioner's life. The emerald always gives a yes to everything.

Fossil Agate

A great stone for financial questions. Fossil agate also indicates more money coming, usually via a job or change of career, and can also signify a promotion. However, its appearance can also indicate the money coming via gambling or an unexpected gift of money. If it appears in a reading, buy a lottery ticket.

Green Jasper

Another jasper, but this stone means neglect or rejection in any area of life—career, love, family, or relationships. In a question, the answer of this stone is very negative and is a clear no.

Iron Pyrite

This stone is sometimes referred to as fool's gold, and as such can indicate a foolish person who is gullible. In a reading, it is telling the questioner to be wary and watchful of others and not to put too much faith in someone. It is another warning stone with neither a yes nor no answer.

Jade

A positive stone that also brings luck to every enterprise. In a reading, it also indicates a true friend and someone who has your back. In a question, it always gives a yes answer.

Jet

If jet is pulled along with the red jasper, this means unfaithfulness in love and relationships. If pulled on its own, it means deceit, and someone is lying to you. Jet is very much a negative stone and gives a giant no in all questions.

Labradorite

This stone tells of a journey and travel, usually overseas, and can indicate a foreign love affair or relationship for the future or present. It is a stone of movement and is a good, happy, positive stone that says a resounding yes in any question.

Moonstone

A great stone for divination and scrying. In a specific crystal reading, it indicates success in all creative ventures and enterprises, especially if setting up a business in the creative field. A stone that gives a yes answer in any specific questions asked.

Opal

This is a rather negative stone to pull as it indicates a specific change, including the ultimate transitional experience—the death of the physical body. In a question, if the opal makes an appearance, it is always a total no.

Pink Jasper

A great stone of finance and one that indicates the questioner will be coming into money or financial benefit. It can also indicate an inheritance, a legacy, or an unexpected gift. In a question-and-answer reading, pink jasper signifies a giant yes.

Red Jasper

This stone indicates someone who is worried and has a troubled mind. If pulled in a reading, it refers to love and the deep emotions associated with it, such as jealousy and lust. It is a stone that comes with a warning and gives neither a firm yes nor no; it is precisely a warning to tread carefully.

Rose Quartz

Another firm favourite in a reading and indicates a lot of healing—either the questioner needs healing or someone around them requires healing. Interestingly though, this stone is also known as the healer's stone, so it can indicate that the questioner is a natural healer, such as a nurse or doctor. A positive yes stone to any questions.

Ruby

Ruby can indicate someone who seeks perfection in everything and can be rather difficult to be around. Further, it can indicate the appearance of a stranger who could be influential but also rather negative. Although with a question, the ruby always gives a positive yes.

Sapphire

I love this stone in a reading as it is so powerful and indicates good fortune, good luck, and peace and harmony—a truly wonderful stone. However, this stone during a reading can also indicate that a mistake from the past is about to catch up with the questioner. Although within general questions, it always gives a yes answer.

Sardonyx

A perfect stone for lovers and indicates a wedding, although not necessarily for the questioner—it just means a wedding is on the horizon. It signifies all positivity in love relationships and good times. A very big yes for everything.

Tektite

A rather negative stone that can indicate someone suffering with depression who needs professional help. This stone gives a definitive no in all questions.

Tiger's Eye

A wonderful stone of protection but in a reading means awareness and a change of direction. This is a stone of the crossroads whereby the person involved in the reading is about to experience a major change in life. However, it is an incredibly positive stone and always means a firm yes in any question. The change in life will always be for the better.

Topaz

Topaz in a reading is another warning stone and indicates an accident, so be wary with driving and travelling. It is telling the questioner to always be on their guard for the forthcoming month. The topaz is a no to any question.

Turquoise

A great positive stone that gives a resounding yes answer to any question asked. In a reading, it indicates contentment and peace in all family relationships, including love and career.

EXAMPLE CRYSTAL READING

There are several ways to perform a crystal reading. One of them is very simple: If you have a question or a query, close your eyes, think of it, and pull out a stone from the bag. Read the meaning of the crystal to see how it answers your question.

The other way is laying all the crystals out on a mat or tray in a line, closing your eyes, and moving your right hand over them. When you feel a tingly or warm sensation in your fingers or palm, stop and pick up that stone. Pick out six. Lay those six stones out in the order they were picked, starting from left to right.

For example, if I perform a general reading for the next three to six months and I pick moonstone, jade, jet, amethyst, sapphire, and turquoise, my reading is very positive. It shows a happy and contented time with a perfect work-life balance. Furthermore, it is also showing me the potential to create something unique and entrepreneurial, that the opportunity to begin a new business venture will be successful, but the choice is mine. However, it is also telling me that there is someone close to me who does not have my best interests at heart and could be lying regarding a situation. Therefore, there is also a warning within that reading.

SUMMARY

Divinatory readings are a wonderful way to interact with crystals, and the more you practice and perform readings, the more you will begin to understand the power and potential within each crystal. There are many stones to choose from and all have their own unique emphasis and will bring a different meaning to a reading. There may be a stone you are particularly attached to and does not feature in my list, but as I have always said, add your own unique type of magic to the list and find your own set of crystals. Remember, magic is of your own making.

The Last Word

As we have seen throughout this book, crystals embody within them the legends and history of the world, and when working with them, we cannot forget this. Their power holds no bounds, and if we use them correctly, our energy can be enhanced, and we can do great good in this world.

Crystals and hedgewitchery are entwined in an eternal way that embodies the central basics of our belief system. What you must remember is that hedgewitchery is primarily concerned with energy and the transformation of energy into one form or another. Everything is in a continual dance of transformation into one form flowing into another; nothing stays the same and, applying the rules of correspondence, we direct that transformation into something else and where we want it to be. The use of crystals within that transference becomes a fundamental practice within hedgewitchery.

Remember, this is your magical practice, and like I always say, change and adapt whatever you need to; the spells and practices contained in this book can be adapted to suit your needs and requirements. Always remember, energy stems from you, and you alone have the choice to do whatever you will with it, but always make sure your actions and intentions stem from love.

Blessed be and keep safe,

Tudorbeth

Appendix of Crystal Spells

In addition to the crystals already discussed, here is an A–Z of crystals and their properties. Use these crystals in your magical practice and daily life; treat them and cleanse and consecrate them to help you connect to the magic of the universe and our magnificent earth. These are the magical and healing areas the crystals can be used for.

Action—Fire Agate, Vesuvianite
Alchemy—Merlinite
Ambition—Manifestation Quartz
Anti-Frustration—White Howlite

Assertiveness—Tiger's Eye

Balance—Heliodor

Barriers—Gateway Quartz

Beauty—Pearl

Calm—Soapstone

Career—Blue Jasper

Change—Metamorphosis Quartz, Fulgurite

Communication—Lapis Lazuli, Peach Aventurine, Honey
   Calcite, Lodalite

Competitiveness—Goldstone

Confidence—Desert Rose, Star Sapphire, Peach
   Aventurine, Yellow Jasper

Creativity—Desert Rose, Fire Opal

Dreams—Manifestation Quartz

Emotions—Chlorite Phantom Quartz

Empaths—Ocean Jasper

Energy—Thunder Egg, Garnet, Water Agate

Enterprise—Fulgurite

Excitement—Meteorite Gibeon

Expansion—Aqua Aura, Blue Goldstone

Extraterrestrial—Moldavite

Family—Tree Agate

Fantasy—Stone of Atlantis

Fertility—Lava

Friendships—Moss Agate

Ghosts—Phantom Quartz, Spirit Quartz

Happiness—Poppy Jasper

Health—Blue Quartz, Chlorite Phantom Quartz

Hex-Breaking—Silver Leaf Agate

Hibernation—Cloud Agate

Higher Power—Angelite

Ideas—Yellow Jasper

Inequality—Blue Jasper

Ingenuity—Blood Agate

Integrity—Fire Agate

Intuition—Star Crystal

Journeys—Falcon's Eye

Justice—Blue Jasper

Leadership—Blue Goldstone

Love—Rose Quartz, Ruby Star, Orange Calcite

Luck—Amber, Tangerine Quartz

Magic—Merlinite, Stone of Atlantis

Magnetic—Haematite

Marriage—Aqua Aura

Meditation—Angel Aura

Mediumship—Star Sapphire

Messenger—Angelite

Money—Moss Agate

Moods—Aquamarine, Water Agate

Motivation—Fire Agate, Vesuvianite

Networking—Honey Calcite

New Beginnings—Nebula Quartz, Yellow Fluorite

Obstacles—Amber

Out-of-Body Experiences—Falcon's Eye

Paranormal—Spirit Quartz

Passion—Heliodor, Orange Calcite

Patience—Snow Quartz, Ocean Jasper

Peace—Ocean Jasper

Perfection—Ruby Star

Perseverance—Snow Quartz

Positivity—Fulgurite, Yellow Fluorite

Possibility—Aqua Aura

Power—Thunder Egg, Gold Sheen Obsidian, Garnet, Scottish Sapphire

Appendix of Crystal Spells

Promotion—Manifestation Quartz

Protection—Turquoise, Galaxite, Garnet

Psychic Awareness—Star Crystal

Relief—Bismuth

Remembrance—Connemara Marble

Sex—Orange Calcite, Lava

Soothe—Soapstone

Stability—Bismuth

Stamina—Snakeskin Agate, Blood Agate

Strength—Amethyst, Fire Opal

Stress-Free—White Howlite, Blood Agate

Struggles—Peach Moonstone, Lodalite

Success—Clear Quartz, Goldstone, Orange Aragonite

Survival—Rock Salt

Talents—Tangerine Quartz

Technology—Haematite

Temper Tantrums—Aquamarine

Toxicity—Petrified Wood

Transformation—Petrified Wood

Travel—Falcon's Eye, Cloud Agate

Truth—Jet, Honey Calcite

Unpredictability—Meteorite Gibeon

Visualisation—Scottish Sapphire

Wealth—Gold Sheen Obsidian

Weight—Peach Moonstone

Wizard—Merlinite

Wonder—Stone of Atlantis

References

Binney, Ruth. *Wise Words & Country Ways: Weather Lore.* Devon: David & Charles, 2010.

Coredon, Christopher. *A Dictionary of Medieval Terms and Phrases.* Woodbridge: D. S. Brewer Publishers, 2007.

Day, Brian. *A Chronicle of Folk Customs.* London: Octopus Publishing Group, 1998.

Eason, Cassandra. *The New Crystal Bible.* London: Carlton Books, 2010.

Forty, Jo. *Classic Mythology.* London: Grange Books, 1999.

Harding, Mike. *A Little Book of the Green Man.* London: Aurum Press, 1998.

Leland, C. G. *Aradia: Gospel of the Witches.* London: David Butt, 1899.

Mathews, John. *The Quest for the Green Man.* Wheaton: Quest Books, 2001.

Moorey, Teresa. *The Fairy Bible.* London: Octopus Publishing Group, 2008.

O'Rush, Claire. *The Enchanted Garden.* London: Random House, 2000.

Palmer, Martin, and Nigel Palmer. *Sacred Britain: A Guide to the Sacred Sites and Pilgrim Routes of England, Scotland, and Wales.* London: Piatkus, 1997.

Radin, Dean. *Real Magic: Ancient Wisdom, Modern Science, and a Guide to the Secret Power of the Universe.* Listening Library, 2018.

Tudorbeth. *The Hedgewitch's Little Book of Seasonal Magic.* Woodbury, MN: Llewellyn Publications, 2022.

———. *The Hedgewitch's Little Book of Spells, Charms & Brews.* Woodbury, MN: Llewellyn Publications, 2021.

TO WRITE TO THE AUTHOR

If you wish to contact the author or would like more information about this book, please write to the author in care of Llewellyn Worldwide Ltd. and we will forward your request. Both the author and the publisher appreciate hearing from you and learning of your enjoyment of this book and how it has helped you. Llewellyn Worldwide Ltd. cannot guarantee that every letter written to the author can be answered, but all will be forwarded. Please write to:

Tudorbeth
℅ Llewellyn Worldwide
2143 Wooddale Drive
Woodbury, MN 55125-2989

Please enclose a self-addressed stamped envelope for reply,
or $1.00 to cover costs. If outside the U.S.A., enclose
an international postal reply coupon.

Many of Llewellyn's authors have websites with additional information and resources. For more information, please visit our website at http://www.llewellyn.com.

TO WRITE TO THE AUTHOR

If you wish to contact the author or would like more information about this book, please write to the author in care of Llewellyn Worldwide Ltd. and we will forward your request. Both the author and the publisher appreciate hearing from you and learning of your enjoyment of this book and how it has helped you. Llewellyn Worldwide Ltd. cannot guarantee that every letter written to the author can be answered, but all will be forwarded. Please write to:

Tudorbeth
℅ Llewellyn Worldwide
2143 Wooddale Drive
Woodbury, MN 55125-2989

Please enclose a self-addressed stamped envelope for reply,
or $1.00 to cover costs. If outside the U.S.A., enclose
an international postal reply coupon.

Many of Llewellyn's authors have websites with additional information and resources. For more information, please visit our website at http://www.llewellyn.com.